The Utopian Dilemma

MURRAY FRIEDMAN is Middle Atlantic states director of the American Jewish Committee. He holds a Ph.D. in American history from Georgetown University and is currently adjunct lecturer on "The American Jewish Experience" at St. Joseph's University in Philadelphia. His books include *Jewish Life in Philadelphia 1830-1940*, *Overcoming Middle Class Rage*, and *New Perspectives on School Integration*.

MICHAEL NOVAK holds the George Frederick Jewett Chair for Public Policy Research at the American Enterprise Institute, Washington, D.C. His books include *The Spirit of Democratic Capitalism* and *Confession of a Catholic*.

The Utopian Dilemma

*American Judaism
and Public Policy*

Murray Friedman

Foreword by Michael Novak

Ethics and Public Policy Center
Washington, D.C.

THE ETHICS AND PUBLIC POLICY CENTER, established in 1976, conducts a program of research, writing, publications, and conferences to encourage debate on domestic and foreign policy issues among religious, educational, academic, business, political, and other leaders. A nonpartisan effort, the Center is supported by contributions (which are tax deductible) from foundations, corporations, and individuals. The authors alone are responsible for the views expressed in Center publications. The founding president of the Center is **Ernest W. Lefever.**

Library of Congress Cataloging in Publication Data
Friedman, Murray, 1926-
  Utopian dilemma.
  Includes index.
  1. Jews—United States—Politics and government. 2. Judaism—United States. 3. Judaism and social problems. 4. Afro-Americans—Relations with Jews. 5. United States—Politics and government—1945- 6. United States—Ethnic relations. I. Title.
E184.J5F77   1985   305.8'924'073   85-7068
ISBN 0-89633-092-3
ISBN 0-89633-093-1 (pbk.)

Clothbound edition, **$12,** *available from:*
Ethics and Public Policy Center
1030 Fifteenth Street N.W., #300
Washington, D.C. 20005

Paperbound edition, **$7.95,** *distributed by:*
Seth Press
P.O. Box 1370
Bryn Mawr, Pennsylvania 19010

© **1985 by the Ethics and Public Policy Center.** All rights reserved.
Printed in the United States of America.

Contents

Foreword *by Michael Novak* vii

Acknowledgments ix

1 Why American Jews Speak to the World 1
    Jewish Liberalism *2*
    Historical Roots *7*
    Jewish Civic Bodies *8*
    Jewish Religious Bodies *10*
    Conservative Judaism *14*
    Religious Orthodoxy *15*
    Public Policy Decisions *16*

2 The Golden Age of American Jewry (1945-1965) 18
    International Public Policy Moves *20*
    McCarthyism *21*
    Social Welfare and Economic Justice *21*
    Civil Rights *23*
    The War on Poverty *28*
    Separation of Church and State *28*
    Resurgence of Orthodoxy *31*

3 An Age of Anxiety (1965-1980) 36
    The Race Revolution *37*
    The Jewish Response *39*
    Rising Crime *42*
    The Jewish Left *43*
    School Desegregation *44*
    Racial Quotas *45*
    Welfare Reform *46*
    Class Conflict *47*
    Israel *49*
    Viet Nam *50*
    An Age of Anxiety *54*

(Continued on next page)

4 New Stirrings (1975-1984)   57
    New Ideological and Political Stirrings *58*
    The Education Morass *61*
    Reexamination of Life-styles *62*
    The Jewish Response *63*
    The Welfare State *64*
    Social Justice Concerns *67*
    The New Right *71*
    Abortion *72*
    Prayer and Bible-Reading *75*
    Human Rights Abroad *77*
    National Defense *80*
    Nuclear Freeze Proposal *83*

5 The Utopian Dilemma   87
    The Jewish Tradition *88*
    The Utopian Dilemma *89*
    Jews and Power *92*
    New Jewish Thought *93*
    Impact on Behavior *96*

Notes   99

Index of Names   109

Foreword

By Michael Novak

MURRAY FRIEDMAN IS a man of unusual fairness, insight, and quiet wisdom. In assessing the role of American Jews in American public life from World War II until today, Dr. Friedman gives broad evidence of all these virtues. He treats with sensitivity the three major Jewish traditions (Orthodox, Conservative, Reform) and the major Jewish agencies and organizations. He examines both religious and secular facets of Jewish life and provides a brief history of the main arguments among Jews about public policy since World War II. By a kind of refraction, his essay sheds much light on the inner struggle of our country to define itself anew, as a free society must necessarily do in every generation.

Any Christian who begins to learn the ways of American Jews through first-hand experience or through books such as this one comes constantly to the edge of amazement. No other American community seems to nourish so much talent, such keen organizational skills, and so vital and articulate an internal diversity. Although Christians speak of "Christian charity," the philanthropic contributions of Jews are truly staggering. In almost every worthy cause, Jewish and non-Jewish, Jewish contributions—and, often, leadership—have few if any rivals. Perhaps more than any other people, American Jews seem to have mastered the secrets both of personal achievement and of a broad range of social and organizational skills.

Midge Decter has said that "the Jews constitute a profound mystery at the center of Western civilization." For Christians, the history of the Jews is somehow normative; the Hebraic roots of Western civilization are for them deeper by far than its Hellenic roots. And the two great religions, Judaism and Christianity, share in monotheism an idea of decisive importance to human universality. Yet Christians vary greatly in their ethnic identities; Jews possess both a common faith and a common ethnicity. Thus, each community faces the conundrum of "the one and the many" from a different starting point.

As Irving Kristol has pointed out, the relation of Jews to this world and to the things of this world is also different from that of Christians. I have always found refreshing a Jewish frankness and directness about worldly success, compared with the odd ambivalence that such success tends to evoke in devout Christians. Jews seem to be both comfortable with success and singularly generous in using its fruits for the betterment of others. As Reinhold Niebuhr observed some four decades ago, the Jewish dedication to social justice, compassion, and civic virtue makes Christians pause in admiration.

Closer to immediate events, the watchful observer of American life cannot be unaware of a recently developing crisis in the American Jewish community, a crisis on which Dr. Friedman sheds needed light. On the one hand, a majority of American Jews seems still to cherish a certain idealism, perhaps a sort of this-worldly hope and perfectionism. On the other hand, "progressive" causes seem so often these days—somewhat ironically—to carry with them a certain threat, not least to specifically Jewish values and interests. From this conflict has grown a new vision among those American Jews called (not quite accurately) "neoconservatives," who sharply question the traditional Jewish allegiance to the fifty-year-old liberal agenda.

This conflict cannot properly be described as one between left and right, between liberals and conservatives. It is, actually, a sharp debate over which path leads best to a just and free society. It is a battle over ideas about the *future*. Dr. Friedman shrewdly interprets this conflict as one between a kind of traditional utopianism and a kind of pragmatic realism. A disagreement over what is properly universal and what is properly particular is no small part of the controversy.

The beauty of America is that, despite the immense range of those things that we hold in common, we each learn much from the almost inarticulate differences among our many spiritual traditions. For this reason, Murray Friedman's sensitive and calm assessment of one crucial tradition is valuable for those who wrestle with analogous problems in other traditions. Drawing upon a vast range of both public and fugitive materials, he has produced a study that is bound to be widely and fruitfully debated. All who seek to understand the meaning of America, at this crucial time of almost palpable turning points, will wish to give it their careful attention.

ACKNOWLEDGMENTS

I would like to express appreciation to a number of people for assistance in making this analysis possible. First and foremost, I want to acknowledge the initiative of Ernest W. Lefever, president of the Ethics and Public Policy Center, in persuading me to undertake this project and then lending encouragement at every step in the process. Rabbi Henry Cohen of Beth David Congregation in Philadelphia, Richard Schifter of Washington, D.C., Jonathan Sarner in Cincinnati, and Milton Himmelfarb read an early draft of the manuscript in its entirety and made a number of helpful suggestions. Some of the ideas and materials that appear in this book were developed earlier as articles in the Hebrew magazine *Tefutsot Israel* and in *Commentary*. I am grateful to Daniel J. Elazar, who first got me started in collecting my thoughts on Jewish public policy by inviting me to write the *Tefutsot Israel* piece and who made valuable suggestions. In addition, the following either gave me interviews, discussed aspects of this work with me, or assisted with information or other help:

Rabbi Richard F. Address, regional director, Pennsylvania Council, Union of American Hebrew Congregations

Penny Bar-Noy, executive secretary, Jewish Reconstructionist Foundation

Rabbi Balfour Brickner, senior rabbi, Stephen Wise Free Synagogue, New York

Richard J. Fox, chairman, National Jewish Coalition

Robert A. Fox, past chairman, Philadelphia chapter, American Jewish Committee

Rabbi Irving Greenberg, president, National Jewish Resource Center

Rabbi Joshua Haberman, senior rabbi, Washington Hebrew Congregation

Cyma Horowitz, Jacob Blaustein Library of the American Jewish Committee

Rabbi Moshe Kalodny, archivist, Agudath Israel of America

Rabbi Wolfe Kelman, executive vice president, Rabbinical Assembly

Rabbi Henry D. Michelson, executive vice president, Synagogue Council of America

Martin Raffel, executive director, American Jewish Congress, Philadelphia

Lawrence Rubin, executive director, Jewish Community Relations Council of Greater Philadelphia

Dorothy Sachs, administrative assistant, United Synagogue of America

Rabbi David Saperstein, co-director and counsel, Religious Action Center of Reform Judaism

Norma Schlager, program coordinator, Synagogue Council of America

David Sidorsky, Department of Philosophy, Columbia University

Burton Siegel, associate director, Jewish Community Relations Council of Greater Philadelphia

Rabbi Seymour N. Siegel, executive director, U.S. Holocaust Memorial Council

David Singer, editor, *American Jewish Year Book*

Rabbi Marc Tanenbaum, director of foreign affairs, American Jewish Committee

The views expressed in this book are my own and do not necessarily reflect those of the American Jewish Committee.

CHAPTER ONE

Why American Jews Speak to the World

That unwillingness to deal with politics and power as it is, but only as it thinks it should be, is characteristic of American Jewish political culture.
HENRY FEINGOLD[1]

JUDAISM ENJOYS AN honored place in American life. On official occasions, such as the inauguration of a president or the dedication of a new school, a rabbi frequently joins a Roman Catholic priest and a Protestant minister in helping to celebrate the event. Americans have come to accept this tri-faith symbolism, even though the nation's 5.7 million Jews constitute less than 3 per cent of the U.S. population.

Despite such symbolic recognition, Jews are not simply a religious counterpart of Protestants and Catholics. They are also an ethnic group with almost 4,000 years of history, much of it endured as a persecuted minority. When one wants to know how Protestantism (save for the evangelicals) or Roman Catholicism stands on certain public policy questions, one can turn to the statements of such organizations as the National Council of Churches or the National Conference of Catholic Bishops. Finding a single spokesman for American Jews is much more difficult. The Synagogue Council of America (SCA) serves as a spokesman for the three major branches in Jewish religious life, but even its staunchest supporters would concede that the SCA is not the sole voice of American Jewry. The communal aspect of Jewish life is so strong that it has spawned a bewildering multiplicity of organizations separate from the religious groupings. Indeed, even the religious dimension is so permeated by the group phenomenon that it is often seen as "the public facade for essentially the communal content of Jewish identification."[2]

Given the times, or a particular issue, or just plain happenstance, expressions of Jewish opinion may come not only from the SCA but also from a social welfare organization like B'nai B'rith, a community relations group like the American Jewish Committee, a pro-Israel organization like the World Zionist Organization–American Section, or a Jewish "defense" organization like B'nai B'rith's Anti-Defamation League (ADL). Or, because of the leading role played by Jews in the science, art, and entertainment worlds, an important expression of opinion may come from an Albert Einstein, a Leonard Bernstein, or a Norman Lear impelled to speak out on various issues using the "Jewish tradition" as his guide.

Who speaks for Jews, then, is perennially debated in the Jewish community.[3] This writer does not possess the daring to attempt to answer the question unequivocally. The best that can be done here is to concentrate on a few of the key groups—namely, the major community relations organizations, operating jointly through the National Jewish Community Relations Advisory Council (NJCRAC), and the three major religious groupings, along with the SCA.

Jewish Liberalism

With respect to politics, Jews have been a quintessentially liberal group. For almost 200 years they have been closely associated with reform movements and even radical groups seeking to improve conditions in our society, better the life of the disadvantaged and discriminated against, and achieve peace. The connections between Jews and the U.S. labor and socialist movements earlier in the twentieth century, and between Jews and the Democratic party beginning in the 1930s, are well known. Even as they became more integrated and affluent, Jews retained their concern for people who suffered discrimination or poverty.[4]

This concern has continued in a period of generally greater conservatism. A survey of Jewish opinion in 1981 found Jews more likely than other segments of the population to support the right of homosexuals to teach in public schools (67 per cent compared to 45 per cent) and government funding for abortion (52 per cent compared to 45 per cent). Although Jews are among the most affluent groups in the population (and thus receive fewer government benefits), a majority (58 per cent versus 35 per cent) was opposed to major cuts in social spending. Simultaneously, those with clear-cut opinions (49 per cent versus 33 per cent) rejected the Reagan administration's call for substantial increases in defense spending. It is only when Jewish interests are seen to be directly involved—for example, by affirmative action programs which include quotas that threaten to exclude Jews from jobs, or when a U.S. administration sells sophisticated weapons to an Arab country—that Jews become somewhat less liberal. But even this does not prevent Jews from approving, to a greater extent than non-Jews, such measures as outright quotas (20 per cent compared to 10 per cent) and school busing for racial integration (23 per cent compared to 12 per cent).[5]

At a time when many other groups have shifted toward the Right, Jews have proved to be the least likely of all white groups to do so. This is best seen in how they vote. Exit polls during the 1982 elections show that in areas where referenda were held on the nuclear freeze issue, as many as 90 per cent of the Jews who went to the polls voted in favor of a freeze. Jews also are the least likely of all religious and ethnic groups to let the race of candidates influence the way they vote. In the California gubernatorial race in November 1982, for example, the percentage of the Jewish vote for the black Democratic candidate, Mayor Thomas Bradley of Los Angeles, was a whopping 75 per cent. Jewish support for the black mayoral candidates Harold Washington in Chicago and W. Wilson Goode in Philadelphia was vital to the success of those two men. And when a dynamic—but conservative—Jewish Republican, Lewis Lehrman, ran for governor of New York in 1982, Jews gave a thumping 64 per cent of their votes to the Democratic winner, Mario Cuomo. While the percentage of the Jewish vote for Reagan in 1980 was considerably higher than for most previous Republican presidential candidates, the combined Jewish vote for his two opponents (Democrat Jimmy Carter and Independent John Anderson) was close to the 65 per cent cast for George McGovern in 1972.

Various explanations have been put forward to explain Jewish liberalism. It is most often seen as rooted in Jewish tradition and law (halakah). Jewish prophets like Amos and Isaiah sided with the most vulnerable people in their societies and railed against injustice, actions which brought them into conflict with the well-established and powerful.

> Learn to do well [Isaiah declaimed]—seek justice, relieve the oppressed, judge the fatherless, plead for the widow—thy princes are rebellious and companions of thieves; every one loveth bribes, and followeth after rewards; they judge not the fatherless, neither does the cause of the widow come unto them. . . . Zion shall be redeemed with justice, and they that return of her with righteousness.[6]

The Torah placed great emphasis on *tzedaka*—not simply charity, for which there is no word in Hebrew, but righteousness. The Talmud scorned the pursuit of fame, power, and wealth. Moses Maimonides, the thirteenth-century Jewish philosopher-physician, elaborated eight degrees of tzedaka in providing for the needs of the poor. By the Middle Ages, as Rabbi David Saperstein points out, this concept had been expanded, and veritable bureaucracies were created within Jewish communities to care for the specialized needs of their members. This extended to intervention by communal authority into the marketplace to insure fair prices, protection of the rights and safety of workers, and even protection of the environment. The nature and purpose of Judaism, many have believed, is to fulfill the messianic dream of redeeming mankind.[7]

This older view, however, has been challenged recently by a number of scholars. Sarah Bershtel and Allen Graubard argue that rabbinic Judaism "was relentlessly Judeo-centered and communal. . . . There was no thought of bringing these truths to others. . . ." Jewish history, they claim, is free of "such outbursts of revolutionary 'messianic' political-religious fervor as the visionary calls for a world of universal equality and justice by the radical Protestant sects of the English civil war."[8] If the Jewish religious tradition is the basis of Jewish social concern, it is said, those who remain closest to the tradition today, namely Orthodox Jews, would be the strongest liberals. But as their voting patterns and the positions they have taken on public policy issues in recent years indicate, this is not the case.[9]

Others have argued that Jewish liberalism is rooted, instead, in the social circumstances in which Jews have found themselves. During the upheaval brought about by the Enlightenment and the French Revolution, it was the liberal Left that championed the emancipation of the Jews; conservative elements opposed it. Conservatives generally felt that citizens, and the state itself, must be Christian. Jews were drawn to the Left but, alarmed by the radical leftist wing that demanded total assimilation, most often ended up on the side of the moderate Left.[10]

Jews adopted from the Enlightenment not only various liberal sociopolitical responses (such as support for internationalism, civil liberties, and social welfare) but also an optimistic faith "that the application of human intellect can create a constantly progressing, universal, cosmopolitan society. . . ."[11] The nineteenth and twentieth centuries saw the emergence of secular Jewish prophets who developed this idea further. Chief among them were Karl Marx, who argued that the social environment could be changed by a triumphant proletariat, and Sigmund Freud, who believed that the psychic environment could be mastered as well.[12]

The hostility of many societies toward Jews has caused Jews to try to change such societies, to make them more open to Jews and other outsiders. The extraordinary passion with which upper-class (and later working-class) Jews attacked racial segregation in the United States, Hasia Diner argues, came from working out "certain tensions of acculturation." Concerned that they would look too self-serving if they fought only against anti-Semitism, many Jews sought integration into American society by joining in middle-class progressive efforts on behalf of blacks and other minorities.[13] Jewish liberalism, Steven M. Cohen says, "should be seen as a reflection (if not, sometimes, a strategy) of the entry and integration of Jews into modern society."[14]

Nevertheless, Seymour Siegel believes that the Jewish tradition has been profoundly misunderstood. It is, he argues, basically conservative. Contemporary liberalism has "a tendency to favor liberty over order," whereas Judaism "has a high esteem for the virtue of order." Liberalism tends "to favor government intervention over private initiative," he says, while Jews "thrive under conditions of opportunity, openness, and freedom rather than under economic control or centralized planning." Liberalism has "a tendency to favor universal characteristics over particularistic ones. . . . [Liberals] therefore tend to downgrade nationalism, ethnic self-identification (except for blacks), and endogamy (marriage within a group)." This leads to a view that all people are basically alike, and that it is wrong to accentuate the elements that make them different.[15]

It should be clear from the foregoing that it is neither possible nor necessary for our purposes here to adjudicate the various claims as to the origins and nature of Jewish liberalism. In any case, it is a combination of religious beliefs and social circumstances that has created the political culture of Jews. Whatever the origins of this liberalism, it has been and continues to be a powerful emotional force that goes beyond specific issues. At least until recent years, political liberalism has been the secular religion of American Jews. "Having lost the faith that there is a God, but not wanting to give up messianism," Siegel has suggested, "they go into politics."[16]

Nevertheless, the ability to tie liberalism to biblical imperatives accounts, in some measure, for its enormous force among American Jews. As liberalism has come under greater criticism today, it has become popular to sneer at its blind spots and failures. And, indeed, liberalism has provided plenty of opportunities for doing so. It should not be forgotten, however, that liberalism has served as a powerful force for improving the lives and broadening the personal freedom of people not only in this country but throughout the world. Liberalism, including its special Jewish variety, has nothing to apologize for save the unwillingness of many of its adherents to move beyond the formulas that served it well in the past.

It is precisely this issue that this book seeks to address. The thesis to be spelled out in the following pages is that so many of the traditional public policies with which Jews have so long been identified and on which they have lavished their fondest hopes and dreams are no longer appropriate to the new stage of American life or to the society itself on which they are so dependent. Having experienced the trauma of World War II and Hitler's death camps, having witnessed the upheavals of the 1960s only to discover the inadequacies of the welfare state, and having watched the contraction of democratic freedoms throughout the world under the assaults of a Marxist-Leninist Soviet Union and its surrogates, Jews have found it becoming dangerous to continue functioning in the same old ways. An "unwillingness to deal with politics and power as it is, but only as it thinks it should be"—to cite Henry Feingold again—"is characteristic of American Jewish political culture." It is the essence of the "utopian dilemma" that Jews face today. Before developing a more detailed analysis of this argument (particularly in chapters 4 and 5), however, we must explain how Jewish public policies have been shaped and expressed.

Historical Roots

The Jewish labor and socialist movements—the two were frequently indistinguishable—were highly influential in the early part of this century. As outgrowths of the needs of the masses of Jews who flooded into this country with high hopes, only to find grinding poverty and inequality, Jewish unionists and socialists spoke out on a wide variety of issues, including the right to organize trade unions, the excesses of unbridled capitalism, and racial and religious discrimination. They also experimented with a number of social welfare ideas and programs that ultimately became a part of the contemporary welfare state. "The union hall began to play the same function that the beth hamidrosh (house of worship) had played in the shtetel (small town in Eastern Europe)," writes Henry Feingold. "Instead of the revered rebbe, there was now the socialist intellectual labor organizer; instead of Torah, there was the doctrine of socialism; and instead of mitzvot (good deeds), there was the struggle to improve the conditions of the underclass."[17]

Another strong factor in the growth of Jewish liberalism was the somewhat amorphous group that Irving Howe has called "the New York intellectuals."[18] ("They have a fondness for ideological speculation, they write literary criticism with a strong social emphasis, they revel in polemic, they strive self-consciously to be 'brilliant,' and by birth or osmosis they are Jews.") Although largely alienated from their Jewish roots and addicted to Left-wing solutions, they were very much a part of the Yiddish and Jewish culture of the times. Many were connected with small but influential publications like *Partisan Review,* the early *Commentary,* and, later, *Dissent* and *Encounter.* "I wonder if anyone has ever properly accounted for the educational significance of such magazines," Joseph Epstein has written.[19] From these magazines and their leading writers, such as Michael Harrington, Paul Goodman, C. Wright Mills, Harold Rosenberg, and Dwight MacDonald, Epstein and many other Jews learned their revulsion to capitalism.

Jewish Civic Bodies

It has been largely through a network of Jewish civic and religious organizations that the formal positions taken by the Jewish community on a wide variety of issues have been transmitted. Jewish community relations agencies have played an especially important role here because of the central place that the battle against prejudice and discrimination has had in American Judaism and the considerable resources and energy that Jews have poured into this battle.

The American Jewish Committee (AJC), organized in 1906, has perhaps been the most influential of these groups. Composed initially of upper-class and more integrated German-Jewish elements, the AJC has fought vigorously to protect the rights of Jews. And soon after its establishment, it began to attack discrimination against blacks, Roman Catholics, and other minorities as well. On broader public policy issues, however, its leadership was quite conservative. Louis Marshall, who guided the organization as its president from 1912 to 1929—it was said of him that American Jewry lived under "Marshall Law"—feared the growing power of the state over the individual and opposed federal laws dealing with child labor, lynching, and the minimum wage.

Because the AJC concentrated its attention at first on threats to Jews in foreign countries, the Anti-Defamation League (ADL) of B'nai B'rith was founded in 1913 to focus on the growing danger to American Jews arising from the Ku Klux Klan, religious stereotyping, and other forms of anti-Semitism. The formation of the American Jewish Congress in 1918 as a third "defense" organization reflected the dissatisfaction of many Jews from Eastern European backgrounds with the leadership of upper-class Jews and the coolness the latter displayed toward Zionism and Jewish nationalism generally.

By the late 1930s and early 1940s, amid the sufferings of the Great Depression and the rise of Naziism in Europe, the older generation of leaders was passing from the scene, and full-time professionals took charge of the Jewish defense organizations. Among them were lawyers, social workers, and social psychologists—men like John Slawson of the American Jewish Committee, Benjamin Epstein and Arnold Forster of the ADL, and Alexander Pekelis, Will Maslow, and

Leo Pfeffer of the American Jewish Congress. Unlike their predecessors, these men had East European origins and had experienced poverty and discrimination firsthand in the United States. With a more equalitarian orientation, they were anxious to collaborate with a wider cross-section of the Jewish community. "One cannot do things *for* the Jewish people; one must do it *with* the Jewish people," Slawson declared at the AJC's 1944 annual meeting. This was a far cry from the approach of the earlier leaders, which had essentially been one of stewardship. But the main thrust of the new leadership was not inward but outward, toward the realization of an ideal American society in which prejudice, discrimination, and intolerance would have no place. This thrust became, in the words of Stephen Isaacs, "an almost religio-cultural obsession."

In retrospect, it can be seen that this idealism was strongly molded by a liberal Left ideology. In a 1945 essay entitled "Full Equality in a Free Society," for example, Alexander Pekelis said that "American Jews will find more reasons for taking an affirmative attitude toward being Jews as members of an organized movement, if they are part and parcel of a great American and human force working for a better world . . . whether or not the individual issues touch directly upon so-called Jewish interests. The tradition and fate of [Jews] are indissolubly bound to those of the forces of liberalism."[20] It was not until the last half of the 1960s that the "utopian dilemma" was recognized.

The work of the Jewish organizations now took on renewed emotional intensity in going beyond protecting the civic and religious rights of Jews to battling on behalf of human rights and economic justice. To many of the new Jewish professionals, and to Jews generally, the Great Depression had demonstrated the need to curb the excesses of an unbridled capitalism. Hence, they saw a need to expand the role of the federal government in providing support and services for those at the bottom of the social and economic scale. By the 1960s, this came to mean broadened support for federally sponsored anti-poverty programs. Although not especially noted at the time, the work of Jewish organizations in helping to create an American version of the welfare state reflected Jewish distrust of the private enterprise system as an equitable means of distributing the rewards of society. The title of a book by Carey McWilliams that was popular in Jewish civil rights circles in the late 1940s—*A Mask For Privilege: Anti-Semitism in America*—caught this mood. Prejudice was ascribed to the wealthier elements in society.

During and immediately after World War II, these organizations (together with other groups, like the Jewish Labor Committee and the Jewish War Veterans of the U.S.A.) enlarged their staffs and activities. They were joined by a network of local Jewish community relations councils that led the battle against bigotry and on behalf of human rights at the local level. The threat posed by the rise and military triumphs of Naziism in Europe called for an all-out assault. In 1944 the national and local groups, together with the major religious organizations, formed the National Community Relations Council—now the National Jewish Community Relations Advisory Council and hereafter referred to as the NJCRAC—to coordinate efforts on the national and local levels. The members of the NJCRAC now include some eleven national and 111 local Jewish organizations. Each year, representatives of these groups hold a meeting whose results are embodied in a Joint Program Plan which reflects, as nearly as anything can, the consensus of the Jewish community on public policy issues.

As noted earlier, this analysis focuses on NJCRAC positions and those of the major Jewish religious bodies, even though the local federations, the Conference of Presidents of Major American Jewish Organizations, and more recently the American Israel Public Affairs Committee (AIPAC) have become major forces in the Jewish community. AIPAC is primarily involved in lobbying on behalf of Israel, although it also works actively in support of a strong U.S. foreign policy.

Jewish Religious Bodies

As a result of their broader communal connections and comparatively low rate of attendance at worship services, Jews are less likely than Protestants or Catholics to be identified with their religious institutions. Moreover, the traumatic nature of the events involving Jews in the first decades of this century, and later the need to dedicate so much moral and financial energy to rescue and "defense," encouraged a pragmatic view of Jewish life that left less room for religious or spiritual expression. This notwithstanding, the major branches within Judaism, with the exception until recently of the more traditional elements, have attempted to make their views known on major public policy issues. In this respect they may be said to have had a certain advantage over traditional Christianity. Although the latter shares Judaism's social values and commitments, at least until recent times it has stressed the primacy of faith over works.[21] This was not the view of Judaism. "It was the peculiar genius of Jewish religious thought," Reinhold Niebuhr has written, "that it conceived the millennium in . . . worldly terms." This notion found expression in an emphasis on the teachings of the Prophets and on such values as communal responsibility for others. "Judaism," Abba Hillel Silver writes, "did not accept a worship of God which does not involve the service of humanity."[22]

The Jews from Iberian (Sephardic) and Middle European (Ashkenazic) backgrounds who came to the United States during the colonial and early national periods were too small in numbers and too preoccupied with gaining a foothold for themselves, both as individuals and as Jews, to make any impact on public policy. It was not until the arrival of large numbers of Jewish immigrants from Central Europe in the mid-nineteenth century and the establishment of Reform Judaism that the conditions for a Jewish religious presence in such matters were laid. The very nature of Reform Judaism facilitated this. Unlike traditional Judaism, which focused on Jewish law, ritual, and peoplehood, Reform placed its emphasis on ethics and moral values. It was in how Jews related to the world and the people around them that Reform saw the essential meaning of Judaism. "Social justice is Jewish," Abraham Cronbach, professor of social relations at Hebrew Union College, once said.[23]

To some degree, this attitude reflected the success that middle-class Jews found in the United States. "Early Reform Jews, newly admitted to the general society and seeing in this the evidence of a growing universalism, regularly spoke of Jewish purpose in terms of Jewry's service to humanity," Jack B. Spiro has observed.[24] In 1873, a Union of American Hebrew Congregations (UAHC) was formed to serve as the central congregational body of all Jews in the United States, becoming a Reform body several decades later. Six years after its original organization, it was joined by the Central Conference of

American Rabbis (CCAR). But despite Reform Judaism's ideology, it moved into the social action arena very slowly. Dominated by a middle- and upper-class constituency, Reform tended to be given to noble words and cautious behavior. Reform activities in the formative years centered on organized charity and social service. The dynamic recognition of social responsibility in the famous Pittsburgh Platform of 1885, which restructured Reform principles, has been described by one student as "in the nature of a postscript appended by the eloquent force of Rabbi Emil G. Hirsch," a distinguished Reform leader, rather than a "willingness to confront the evils in society."[25] Even in guarding Jewish interests from the inroads of Christian sectarianism in public institutions, Reform was careful. In an address to the CCAR in 1904, Rabbi Joseph Krauskopf of Philadelphia said that Reform should oppose the introduction of the Bible for religious purposes "into institutions which are maintained by the Commonwealth." However, a committee appointed to look into the matter later warned against initiating legal tests. "Defeat in such matters is so baneful," the committee argued, "that the risk of it had rather not be incurred." Instead, Reform gave itself over to a campaign of public education.[26]

American Reform Judaism can hardly be faulted here. Jews were still a small and relatively isolated group who took their cues from the broader Christian culture. At that time the Social Gospel movement within Protestantism was still in its infancy, and the Federal Council of Churches in America (later the National Council of Churches) only proclaimed a social creed in 1908.[27] Although the CCAR did speak out on child labor problems and higher wages for the workingman, its unwillingness to get involved in particular problems remained strong. It was not until 1928 that a comprehensive and bold social program was formulated. This Reform program included all the recommendations of the 1912 social platform of the Federal Council of Churches and the 1919 Bishops' program of the Roman Catholic Church.[28] In addition, the CCAR approved the right of conscientious objection to war and denounced all forms of imperialism.

The Great Depression forced the CCAR to bring its social concerns up to date. In 1930 the conference called for greater appropriations for public works, adoption of a shorter work week, and greater distribution of the profits of industry.[29] The following year the CCAR expressed "deep concern with and a condemnation of conditions which seemed to offer evidence of the inability of the Negro to secure economic or civil justice."[30]

These were the years when a new note began to emerge. Despite Reform Judaism's upper-class character, its statements began to echo the ideology of the Jewish labor and socialist movements. In his presidential address to the CCAR in 1931, Rabbi Morris Newfield went beyond the organization's "unquestioned endorsement of economic liberal reform" to "loudly protest against a system which in the most approved laissez-faire fashion engenders periodically a most tragic culmination of moderate but continuous unemployment conditions." CCAR's Commission on Social Justice asserted that "the government, amid the inactivity or impotence of private industry, must act in a manner to stimulate industry and cause employment."[31]

In subsequent years the CCAR elaborated on this theme. In 1932 the conference held that "all private ownership of natural resources and the machinery of large-scale production [involves] an injustice. . . . An individualistic profit economy is as sinful as it has proved a failure." The CCAR added that "an individualistic, profit-oriented economy is in direct conflict with the ideals of religion." The following year the CCAR declared that it would "welcome the socialization of banking, transportation, and all forms of commercial communication." By the time of U.S. entry into World War II, the CCAR had reached a point where it felt that "the resources of the world belong to all . . . and should be made available to all."[32] The "Jewish question" could be solved only "when the universalistic message of justice and equality was accepted by all." Reform, according to Henry Feingold, was now playing the role of developing an ideology for western Jews that anarchism, socialism, and Russian populism played for their Eastern European brethren, even though it did not have so direct an impact on their actual lives.

The 1930s, it should be recalled, were years of extraordinary trauma for Jews. The response of Reform, like that of other Jews, has to be seen against the background of a collapsing capitalism and the rise of Naziism and Communism in Europe. The move to the left among American Jews was moderate, given the radical solutions being offered elsewhere. Nevertheless, Reform had moved into a militant posture on its path to modernism, a posture that has characterized the movement down to the present time.

Conservative Judaism

Conservative Judaism moved into the public policy arena more slowly than Reform did. The Conservative movement was created at the turn of the century by a coalition of Reform and traditional Jews who were deeply worried about the kind of Judaism that could survive in the United States. The East European Jews who were arriving in great numbers, it was felt, needed a "middle ground" Judaism that captured the emotional texture of Orthodoxy but was less foreign to their life-style than Reform Judaism. Since Conservatism's focus in the United States was on preserving Judaism from the assimilating tendencies of a new environment, the formulation of public policy positions was very low on the agenda of the Rabbinical Assembly, organized in 1900, and the United Synagogue of America, founded in 1913. Indeed, when the Rabbinical Assembly organized its Social Action Commission in 1932, it confessed:

> It is clear that in this area the Reform and Conservative rabbis follow rather than lead the Jewish community, and this is not the case in some Protestant denominations, where the ministers, even if not leaders on social attitudes, generally express social attitudes in advance of their parishioners. . . . Jewish social attitudes derive more from 19th century liberalism and socialism than the Hebrew prophets. . . . It is not easy to see in present-day Jewish social attitudes the heritage of the Jewish religion.[33]

The chairman of the new Social Action Commission declared that its objectives were to formulate and publicize the views of the assembly on the social and economic problems of the times. Two years later, under the chairmanship of Rabbi Milton Steinberg, the Rabbinical Assembly adopted a wide-ranging pronouncement on social justice covering such topics as "the individual and society," "human cooperation," and "the social use of wealth and peace." In somewhat abstract and idealized rhetoric, the assembly said it was seeking a society "in which all men shall be free . . . protected against all forms of oppression and exploitation . . . a social order . . . based on human cooperation rather than competition inspired by greed. . . ."[34] The positions taken by both Reform and Conservative Judaism, Albert Vorspan and Eugene J. Lipman note, stemmed from "the expressed conviction . . . that the profit system of commerce and industry was not completely compatible with their interpretation of reverence for human personality."[35]

In the early period, Conservative Judaism did not succeed in putting down deep roots or building a strong organizational base. But as the United States moved toward World War II, American Judaism was evolving into a kind of ethnic religion where a concern about and commitment to the Jewish people was balanced by a desire for greater integration into the larger society. Thus, in the post–World War II period, Conservative Judaism became an influential current in Jewish religious life.

Religious Orthodoxy

American Orthodox Judaism was the one branch of Judaism that was, by its very nature, most divorced from worldly questions. Unlike Reform and Conservative Judaism, Orthodoxy was (and remains) a highly fragmented movement involving many small synagogues with Yiddish-speaking rabbis, religious organizations like Agudath Israel World Organization and Agudath Israel of America, the National Council of Young Israel, and such educational institutions as Yeshiva University and its affiliate, Rabbi Isaac Elchanan Theological Seminary.

Orthodoxy's energies were given over to keeping Jews aware of the Torah, mainly through ritual and worship. Battling against the blandishments of the broader society that were luring Jews away from the practice of their faith, Orthodoxy was hostile even to cooperation with Reform and Conservative Judaism. The latter two were seen as pale versions of Judaism and, at worst, as Christianized forms. Organizational expression took the form of the Union of Orthodox Jewish Congregations of America (UOJC), founded in 1898, and the organizing of European-trained rabbis into the Agudath Harabbonim, formed in 1902. Nevertheless, a more modern Orthodoxy was evolving. The development of an English-speaking Orthodox rabbinate which "sensed that America was different and certain accommodations or adjustments had to be made" resulted in the establishment in 1935 of a Rabbinical Council of America that was destined to surpass in numbers and influence the Agudath Harabbonim.[36]

Since the basic constituency of Orthodoxy in the first decades of the century tended to be the poorest Jews, one might think that Orthodoxy would have been more liberal on public policy issues. Such liberal tendencies, however, found expression primarily in the secular Jewish organizations. "During the earlier immigrant days," Marshall Sklare has written, Orthodoxy "functioned as a cultural constant in the life of the disoriented newcomer, as a place of haven in the stormy new environment."[37]

Public Policy Decisions

In the first decades of this century the various Jewish religious movements were not significantly involved in public policy issues, notwithstanding the high-blown announcements of Reform Judaism. The pragmatic preoccupation of most Jews was survival. The religious leaders of an immigrant generation that was "pioneering on the urban frontier," in Samuel Lubell's felicitous phrase, were too preoccupied with developing and maintaining their organizations and keeping in touch with their constituents to involve themselves deeply in matters not directly affecting their group. The *History of the United Synagogue, 1913-1963* reports that in the 1920s the organization aided in "kashrut supervision [ritually permitted use and serving of food]; was much involved with the religious life on campus and helped to establish kosher eating facilities for its religious schools."[38] Public policy activities were left in the hands of Jewish social and political movements and, more and more, Jewish philanthropic and community relations organizations, which had more money and larger staffs. It is perhaps symptomatic of this that down to the present time a number of rabbis, beginning with Stephen Wise, have chosen to express their social action concerns through secular Jewish agencies as much as through Jewish religious organizations.

Nevertheless, the conditions for broader Jewish involvement in social policy had been laid. By the 1930s the leaders of the three religious movements were becoming restless at the dominant role assumed by the philanthropic and defense organizations, which, some felt, were not "interested in religion" or "synagogue-minded." These institutions, Bernard Bamburger states, were "administered by lay and professional leaders whose attitude toward the Jewish religion ranged from simple indifference to open hostility."[39]

When the Synagogue Council of America (SCA) was organized in 1926, the purpose was to bring together the three religious branches through their six national lay and rabbinical bodies "for the purpose of enabling them to speak and act unitedly in furthering [the] . . . religious interests they shared in common."[40] The SCA was to become roughly the Jewish equivalent of the National Council of Churches or the National Conference of Catholic Bishops. It should be noted, however, that individual Jewish congregations are basically autonomous, and compliance with resolutions of central bodies like the SCA is voluntary.

From the outset, the SCA concerned itself with specific issues, even though it was not ready to develop a comprehensive platform. The delegates endorsed a federal anti-lynching bill. They also adopted a resolution that dealt with the movies. The resolution praised Christian groups working for less sexually explicit films but called for greater reliance on educating the public instead of censorship. At the height of World War II the SCA joined with the then Federal Council of Churches and National Catholic Welfare Conference in a seven-point platform on the aims of peace, thus helping to create public support for the establishment of the United Nations. The Jewish religious presence was not yet broadly felt, however. Thus, when the United Nations was founded in San Francisco in 1945, several secular Jewish groups were invited to attend, but the SCA was not.[41] It was not until after the war that the energies of religious Judaism were free to play a more significant role in dealing with the central issues facing society.

CHAPTER TWO

The Golden Age of American Jewry (1945-1965)

Equality as a religious commandment means personal involvement, fellowship, mutual reverence and concern. . . .
RABBI ABRAHAM HESCHEL, at the National Conference on Religion and Race, Chicago, January 1963

FORTY YEARS AFTER the fact, it is hard to understand the euphoria that swept through the American Jewish community following the end of World War II. Hitler's death camps had demonstrated how depraved human beings could be, and Jews had suffered beyond belief. Yet the war against Naziism had been won, the creation of the United Nations suggested that the twin scourges of racism and war could finally be ended, and the Jews had established a homeland. American Jews felt they could face the future with optimism, and indeed the next twenty years represent the golden age of American Jewry. It would take until the latter 1960s and the Six-Day War for the enormity of the Holocaust to reassert itself.

In the late 1940s and 1950s, many American cities and states made racial and religious discrimination in employment, education, and housing unlawful. This was followed in the 1960s by federal legislation that further expanded civil rights. By 1965, the National Jewish Community Relations Advisory Council (NJCRAC) said, "the war against legally enforced, sanctioned, or tolerated racial segregation had been won."[1] Meanwhile, Jews watched in fascination as the Second Vatican

Council, which met in Rome 1962 to 1965, condemned anti-Semitism "by anyone at any time." The U.S. economy entered a period of expansion that seemed to be shared by most segments of society, and many domestic problems appeared to be on the road to resolution.

The hopefulness that many Jews felt in the immediate postwar period reflected their own personal experience. Significant numbers of Jews had gained professional skills through higher education and had developed middle-class attitudes. They were therefore prepared to take advantage of the opportunities that opened up as prejudice and discrimination declined. As a result of their newfound prosperity, they were also able to move out of areas of immigrant settlement. Throughout the United States, the *United Synagogue Review* reported, Conservative congregations were formed where none had existed before, and new synagogues were built to meet the growing needs of existing congregations. (By 1970, membership in Conservative congregations was roughly one and a half million, compared with one million in Reform congregations and about three-quarters of a million identifying with Orthodox synagogues.)[2]

The immediate postwar period was a time of religious revival as well as religious growth. Jewish thinkers both past and present like Leo S. Baeck, Franz Rosenzweig, Martin Buber, and Abraham Heschel played a prominent part in this revival. "I owe a debt to Martin Buber, my first sociology teacher," the social critic Amitai Etzioni later declared. "His theories of the 'I-thou' and 'I-it' relationships are the source of my notion of mutuality."[3] But some questioned the authenticity of this Jewish revival, referring to it as "symbolic ethnicity." Their reasons for doing so are perhaps understandable. Religion had indeed become a sign of the social respectability that the broader society seemed to require. Such criticism, however, missed the point. Institutions built for one purpose have the capacity to take on other purposes. As Judaism came increasingly to be seen as the counterpart of Protestantism and Roman Catholicism, and was accorded greater respect by the media, Jews began to take their faith more seriously.[4]

Enough time and distance had elapsed since the immigrant generations for Jews to feel more comfortable in exploring the religious dimensions of group experience.[5] This renewal of interest strengthened the authority of Jewish religious spokesmen. The Synagogue Council of America (SCA), which for a time had been dependent for funding on the Anti-Defamation League and the American Jewish Committee, began to survive on its own, gradually expanding its budget and activities.[6] No longer transfixed by the war, the need to care for refugees, or the creation of the State of Israel, American Jews could turn aside from purely parochial interests and pour an increasing portion of their energies into dealing with general public policy questions.

In this effort, Reform Judaism once again took the lead. Following an impassioned plea by Rabbi Maurice Eisendrath at the 1946 assembly of the Union of American Hebrew Congregations (UAHC), a Joint Commission on Social Action was organized in 1949 in collaboration with the Central Conference of American Rabbis (CCAR). Later reorganized, the commission set out to create social action or community affairs committees in each Reform temple in the United States. A few years later, Conservative Judaism's Rabbinical Assembly and United Synagogue of America also set up a Joint Commission on Social Action and began organizing local study and action groups. Even the Union of Orthodox Jewish Congregations (UOJC) created a Communal Affairs Committee and evidenced growing interest in such activities.

International Public Policy Moves

Strengthening the recently established United Nations was a special Jewish interest. In the early 1950s the CCAR called the United Nations the sole instrument for bringing the peoples of the world into a fellowship of peace and prosperity and wanted it to become "the nucleus of world government." The Rabbinical Assembly called for the evolution of the organization into "a world federation, which would preserve peace through the enforcement of world law." Jewish support for the world body as "the last, best hope for mankind" continued to be strong well into the 1960s.[7]

Closely related to this was the strong backing given by Jewish groups to the Genocide Convention ratified by the U.N. General Assembly in 1948 and submitted to member nations for approval. Hadassah and the ADL, the CCAR, and the Rabbinical Assembly all urged the U.S. Senate in the 1950s to ratify the convention. Reiteration of Jewish support continued throughout the 1960s and 1970s. The Senate, however, has failed to act on the convention, apparently from fear that international authority might impose outside constraints on the functions of the U.S. government or interfere in internal affairs.

Jewish support for the United Nations was also strong during the Korean conflict. When the U.N. Security Council agreed to the use of force to stem North Korea's attack on South Korea in June 1950, both the CCAR and the UAHC promptly announced their support for this action. The former called for a permanent "UN police force capable of taking gradually from separate governments . . . the responsibilities of maintaining order and preventing aggression throughout the world."[8]

McCarthyism

As the Cold War with the Soviet Union deepened in the early 1950s, Jewish religious organizations worried increasingly about what the United Synagogue of America described as "attempts to enforce conformity through such undemocratic means as censorship; loyalty oaths . . . limitations to academic freedom; and the stifling of dissent."[9] Senator Joseph McCarthy, a Republican from Wisconsin, was a particular source of concern. Although he never attacked Jews and, indeed, had several staff members who were Jewish, the percentage of Jews across the religious and civic spectrum who opposed him was twice that of the rest of the nation, according to the polls. McCarthyism threatened "what had become a kind of secular religion for many Jews, a mixture of liberalism and civil libertarianism at home, with reconciliation abroad."[10] The CCAR was especially outspoken in its criticism of McCarthy's tactics, "the practice of imputing guilt merely by association and harassment of religious leaders and others for association with liberal or leftist causes. . . ." In 1954 the CCAR joined in the call "to strip him of his committee chairmanships," and it applauded his censure by the Senate the following year.[11]

Social Welfare and Economic Justice

Once the threat of McCarthyism had been removed, the energies of Jews focused on social welfare. Community surveys developed by the American Jewish Committee (AJC) in the late 1950s and early 1960s found few Jews who believed that belonging to a synagogue and practicing ritual observances were what constituted "the good Jew." Roughly half, however, thought it essential to promote social justice by working for civic betterment, helping the underprivileged, and struggling to achieve equality for blacks.[12] During the Truman and Eisenhower years, Jewish religious leaders focused their efforts on defending the welfare state erected by the New Deal. They opposed the Taft-Hartley and "right-to-work" laws designed to curb union abuses. Even as Jews began to move in larger numbers into middle-class occupations and professions, they retained their attachment to the labor movement. Conservative and Reform rabbis urged the CIO and the AFL to heal the breach in organized labor and rejoiced in 1955 when the two groups merged.[13] They also sought to extend the welfare state. The CCAR called for government action to meet "the grievous need for low-cost housing throughout the country, especially among people in low income categories and war veterans." The UAHC pushed for "medical care . . . at a cost within the reach of all."[14]

So completely had the Jewish community become attached to the welfare state and the liberal agenda that even Orthodox groups found themselves carried along. At its 1951 convention, the Rabbinical Council of America approved resolutions supporting price and rent controls. Following an address three years later by Walter Reuther, head of the United Automobile Workers, the council adopted a resolution calling for a united labor movement and urged Congress to reconsider its opposition to extending federal housing programs. In focusing so heavily on economic justice, Jewish civic and religious groups showed that they had retained their earlier suspicions of private enterprise. While noting Judaism's recognition of the "right to property," Albert Vorspan and Eugene Lipman added that "property and wealth must not be used for evil purposes." They described what they saw as a growing concentration of economic power during and following the war, and warned that "vigilance and concern will be needed on the part of every concerned citizen to maintain America's diversified economic system on a democratic and expanding basis."[15]

Their criticisms were not without merit. Obvious inequities existed. Vorspan and Lipman failed to recognize, however, that it was the very same economic processes that were responsible for the enormous postwar economic expansion, whose results were increasingly enjoyed by so many segments of society, including Jews. It was likely, too, that economic growth laid the basis for human rights expansion as well. It is hard to believe that the civil rights revolution could have made much progress had it been forced to find friends and allies among people competing for scarce or nonexistent jobs and other opportunities.[16]

Civil Rights

In the post–World War II years, Jewish groups focused considerable attention on "the promotion of equality under the law and full equality of opportunity."[17] Not surprisingly, Jewish community relations organizations led an all-out assault on discrimination. It was a measure of their universalistic concerns that they referred to themselves now as community relations agencies rather than "defense" agencies. They saw themselves engaged in an effort to wipe out prejudice and discrimination directed against all excluded groups, not merely Jews. Employing social psychologists who had fled from Nazi Germany, the American Jewish Committee sponsored a series of books under the general heading "Studies in Prejudice." The first volume, *The Authoritarian Personality*, published at the height of the McCarthy era, argued that anti-Semitism was a symptom of a generally abnormal psychological pattern in both individuals and society, while tolerance was not only morally right but psychologically healthy. The AJC also hired a black psychologist, Kenneth B. Clark, to prepare a paper on the impact of segregation for the White House Conference on Children in 1950. Clark's paper, which contended that racial segregation inflicted psychological damage on black children, was subsequently cited by the Supreme Court in a famous footnote to *Brown* v. *Board of Education*, the 1954 decision outlawing racial segregation in the public schools.[18] At this time, too, the ADL mounted country-wide educational campaigns utilizing films and radio and television announcements to emphasize the essential oneness of the human family. The American Jewish Congress, dissatisfied with such "brotherhood sloganeering," concentrated on litigation that would harness the force of government to counter religious and racial discrimination.

Along with church, labor, and black allies, the national Jewish agencies and local community relations councils persuaded city councils and state legislatures to enact various fair employment and fair educational practices and other civil rights measures in the forties and fifties. Black organizations usually played a minor role in these early battles. Indeed, there were signs that some black leaders were becoming irritated, even at that early date, by the prominence of Jews and Jewish groups in matters vitally affecting the black community.[19] By the early 1960s, when the action shifted to the national level and the fight was increasingly taken over by blacks, twenty states and forty cities with about 60 per cent of the U.S. population had some kind of fair employment law, while seventeen states and cities had banned discrimination in the rental and sale of housing. The involvement of Jews and Jewish groups was so strong between 1945 and 1960 that it is probably no exaggeration to say that the period was the "Jewish phase" of the civil rights revolution.

As "sit-ins," "Freedom Rides," and other direct action activities took the spotlight from legal and educational efforts in the early sixties, young and not-so-young Jewish activists traveled into the South in great numbers to participate with blacks in the struggle. It is estimated that Jews made up two-thirds of the white Freedom Riders in the summer of 1961, and about a third to a half of the Mississippi summer volunteers three years later.[20] (So extensive was Jewish participation that satirist Allen Sherman composed a parody sung to the tune of *"Frère Jacques."* "And how's your sister Ida?" "She's a Freedom Rida.")

Jews who travelled to the South often experienced harassment and violence. Two of the three young civil rights workers who were murdered in Neshoba County, Mississippi, were Jews. Many of those who went south were assimilated Jews in rebellion against postwar suburban affluence. Spiritually, however, it could be said that they were wearing their yarmulkas. "Even the very Jewish radical who may ignore his Jewishness is the product of messianic fervor," Rabbi Philip Bernstein said.[21] As the civil rights movement merged with opposition to U.S. involvement in Viet Nam, a group of Jews emerged who sought to use the Jewish religious tradition for "radical and alienated social critiques."[22]

Rabbis and Jewish religious bodies were generally slower to move into civil rights activities than secular Jewish activists, partly because of the primacy and technical competence of the Jewish civic agencies. They also trailed behind Protestant and Roman Catholic groups. Nevertheless, they did begin to enter the picture soon after World War II. In 1946 the Rabbinical Council adopted a resolution opposing violence and discrimination against minorities and dissolution of the federal Fair

Employment Practices Commission as contrary to "Torah and democracy."[23] In 1947 the CCAR commended the creation by President Truman of the President's Committee on Civil Rights—a Reform rabbi, Roland B. Gittelsohn, served as a member—and urged immediate implementation of the committee's recommendations the following year.[24] By the mid-1950s, social action increasingly became the theme of public policy pronouncements by Jewish religious organizations. It was after the Supreme Court handed down its momentous school desegregation decision in 1954 that the Conservative movement created its Joint Commission on Social Action. "We are hopeful," Dr. Bernard Segal, the director of the United Synagogue declared, "that through it we will succeed in conveying to our people a fuller understanding of the universal teachings of our tradition so that these may be translated in the affairs of the general community and the world as well as the Synagogue."[25] As tensions deepened in the South, and isolated Jewish communities in the region hunkered down to ride out the storm, a courageous group of rabbis emerged, including Emmett Frank in Virginia, Perry Nussbaum in Mississippi, Charles Mantinband in Alabama, and Jacob Rothschild in Georgia. In spite of threats and actual bombings, these men called for peaceful accommodation to school integration.[26]

It was the National Conference on Religion and Race, held in 1963 and convened by the Department of Racial and Cultural Relations of the National Council of Churches, the Social Action Department of the National Catholic Welfare Conference, and the Synagogue Council, that brought about a more significant involvement by synagogues and rabbis in the struggle for civil rights.[27] A religious commemoration of the centennial of the Emancipation Proclamation in Chicago attracted 657 delegates from all parts of the nation. The delegates heard the Rev. Martin Luther King, rapidly becoming the unquestioned leader of the civil rights revolution, describe religious leaders as the "chief moral guardians of the community." He chided them, however, for failing to be "faithful to their prophetic mission."[28]

The opening address at the conference was delivered by Rabbi Abraham Heschel, professor of Jewish ethics and mysticism at the Jewish Theological Seminary in New York. Heschel embodied the Jewish conscience. A student of Chasidism who had written a book called *The Prophets,* Heschel had come to this country as a refugee from Nazi Germany in 1939. Ironically, he was first discovered by Protestant and Catholic leaders who sought his advice on theological and social issues.[29] He was increasingly to become the "address" to which the White House, the Pope, the activists, the theologians, and American Jews themselves turned when they required a Jewish spokesman.[30] Heschel electrified his 1963 audience by noting at the outset of his remarks that at the "first conference" on religion and race "the main participants were Pharaoh and Moses." He told his audience that "racism is man's gravest threat to man. . . . How many disasters do we have to go through in order to realize that all of humanity has a stake in the liberty of one person; whenever one person is offended, we are all hurt."

Heschel introduced a somewhat different note in the Jewish view of public policy. His ideas were rooted in existential Jewish theology. One entered the struggle for human rights through an encounter with God. "The problem is not only how to do justice to the colored people," he thundered; "it is, also, how to stop the profanation of God's name by dishonoring the Negro's name."[31] "By negligence and silence we have all become accessory . . . to the injustice committed against the Negroes by men of our nation. . . ." He declared that the Prophets' great contribution to humanity was the discovery of the *evil of indifference:* "One may be decent and sinister, pious and sinful." Heschel coupled his analysis with a call to action. "Equality as a religious commandment goes beyond the principle of equality before the law. Equality as a religious commandment means *personal involvement, fellowship, mutual reverence and concern. . . .*" Finally, Heschel issued a challenge: "Humanity can thrive only when challenged, when called upon to answer new demands, to reach out for new heights. . . . Imagine how smug, complacent, vapid, and foolish we would be, if we had to subsist on prosperity alone. . . ."[32]

Heschel galvanized the Jewish religious community into direct action on behalf of civil rights. Before he appeared on the scene, only Reform Judaism had played a leading role in such efforts. Heschel made it appropriate, even necessary, for Conservative and Orthodox elements to become involved as well. During the famous march led by Dr. King from Selma to Montgomery, Heschel was a central figure—"Father Abraham," they called him—marching alongside King and Ralph Bunche at the head of the procession.[33]

Thus, a Jewish religious presence became an integral part of the civil rights movement, alongside Protestant and Roman Catholic leaders. The 1963 conference strongly urged Congress to approve the pending omnibus civil rights bill, and Jewish religious bodies turned out their members in great numbers for the March on Washington in the summer of 1963 on behalf of the legislation.[34] Rabbi Joachim Prinz, the head of the American Jewish Congress, who had once been a refugee from Hitler's Germany, was one of the platform speakers. During the following year, seminarians of the three faiths kept a vigil at the Lincoln Memorial until the bill was passed.[35]

Along with Heschel, Dr. King exerted an enormous moral influence on Jews. In 1963 he made a special effort to reach them by attending the conventions of the United Synagogue of America and the UAHC. At the latter he linked his "dream" to the demonstrated ability of Jews to transcend discouragement and despair. And later he wrote that "the lesson of Jewish mass involvement in social and political action is worthy of emulation." Another high point was the Rabbinical Assembly's 1963 convention, when a group of rabbis left the convention hall and went to Birmingham to express their solidarity with King, then in prison.[36] The following year, in response to an appeal by King to the CCAR to join him as a witness "to our joint convictions of equality and racial justice," a group of Reform rabbis went to St. Augustine, Florida, before the Senate vote on the omnibus civil rights legislation. After fifteen of them, along with a layman and three black youths, were jailed for a sit-in at a restaurant, they released a statement that made a classic argument for conscientious objection to unjust laws.[37]

Orthodoxy, now several generations old in the United States, was caught up in this atmosphere. In an address to a Young Israel meeting in New York, Rabbi Aaron Soloveitchik, a leading Talmudic authority, examined civil rights from the perspective of halakah (Jewish law).[38] And during the demonstration in Selma, an Orthodox rabbi from Berkeley was arrested on the Fast Day of Esther. Continuing to fast in jail, he read the Megilla (Book of Esther), with its recitation of the persecution of Jews by "the wicked Haman," to a "captive audience" of two students from Berkeley.

The civil rights movement scored important successes in destroying the institutional structure of segregation and discrimination in the United States. These achievements, however, only moved the struggle to a new and more complicated level. They underlined the basic inequality of blacks and other minorities, as reflected in the ugly social and economic conditions found in the slums of the affluent society. The right of blacks to sit at a lunch counter in the South did not put money in their pockets to pay for the meal.

The War on Poverty

Beginning in the mid-1960s, the Jewish community put an increasing amount of effort into the War on Poverty. In its 1966-67 report the National Jewish Community Relations Advisory Council (NJCRAC) affirmed the Economic Opportunity Act of 1964, whose goal of full employment was to be reached through government programs of improved education, public works, and job training. The NJCRAC added that other foreign or domestic undertakings "must not be allowed to detract from or diminish support of programs for the alleviation of poverty."

The Jewish religious bodies were equally supportive. A 1965 CCAR report on "The War on Poverty" declared:

> We of the CCAR, who have long fought for such social objectives as unemployment insurance, old age pensions, a national health care program, full employment, minimum wages, and Federal aid to education, are happy that our government is implementing its programs for a Great Society of progress and culture from which ignorance, disease, slums, and health-destroying and humiliating poverty shall be eliminated.[39]

By 1969 a political backlash had set in against the War on Poverty. Nonetheless, the Synagogue Council joined other religious denominations in urging Congress to continue its efforts to alleviate poverty and unemployment, while the United Synagogue called for "a federally funded and administered program that would ultimately replace the present welfare system." The belief that solutions could be found to this age-old problem was caught in the title of a publication of the UAHC, *There Shall Be No Poor*.

Separation of Church and State

Closely related to the strong backing given the civil rights movement was a major effort mounted by Jewish groups after World War II on behalf of freedom of religion and the separation of church and state. Once fearful that such activity would bring down on their heads the ire of their Christian neighbors, Jews now had a greater self-confidence that made them more willing to accept such a risk.

Like other stands taken on public policy issues, this one had deep roots in Jewish experience. Postwar American Jewry had come to believe strongly that freedom was safest where, as Rabbi Arthur Hertzberg declared, the dominance of religion in public life had been "blunted."[40] In *The French Enlightenment and the Jews,* Hertzberg argued that the rise of the secular state had been the basis of Jewish emancipation. Coupled with suspicion among Jews about any entanglement of church and state was the deep loyalty and affection they had for public schools, which had served for most of them as the first and foremost institution for their integration in America. Because of past Jewish confrontations with Christianity, most Jews felt that if parochial schools (for which Roman Catholics were now beginning to claim funding from the state) were aided by the government, the United States would become a society of "coexisting ghettos." This would be dangerous for Jews and for other religious "outsiders."

Jewish civic agencies, along with civil libertarian and liberal Protestant groups, moved aggressively in the late forties to remove Christian practices from public places, particularly the schools, and to oppose, legally, efforts to obtain government funding for private and parochial schools. Jewish religious bodies, without the legal talent or perhaps the ideological commitment of the civic agencies, got a later start. In 1948 the Synagogue Council of America and the NJCRAC formed a Joint Committee on Religion and the Public School (later, the Joint Advisory Committee on Religion and the State). It was through this body, guided by Leo Pfeffer, the brilliant head of the American Jewish Congress's Commission on Law and Social Action, that the largest part of Jewish activity on the issue of church-state separation took place. At a series of public conferences, statements were formulated in opposition to released and shared time, religious observances in public schools, and the teaching of religion under the guise of "moral and spiritual values." Even Orthodoxy's Rabbinical Council went along on most of these questions.[41] As the official history of the SCA notes, with only the slightest exaggeration, these positions "can be fairly said to represent the majority opinion, almost the official opinion of American Jewry. . . ."[42]

As in the early stages of the civil rights struggle, Jewish groups played a central role in framing the issues, selecting the cases, and developing the legal arguments that were eventually to win approval from the Supreme Court. Pfeffer, the leading constitutional attorney in the field, argued many cases before the Court and often was consulted by others involved in such litigation.[43]

By the late 1940s a new body of law on church-state relations that reflected a more strict reading of the First Amendment had taken shape. In the so-called New Jersey bus case in 1947 (*Everson* v. *Board of Education*), the Supreme Court asserted that "the clause against establishment of religion was intended to erect 'a wall of separation' between church and state." (Nonetheless, the Court upheld free bus transportation to private and parochial school students as a service to the child.) The "wall of separation" view was reiterated the following year in *McCollum* v. *Board of Education,* and four years later in *Zorach* v. *Clauson.*

Nevertheless, such religious practices as prayer and Bible-reading remained common in public schools. Anxious to find ways around the Supreme Court's unpopular decisions, the New York State Board of Regents proposed a brief "nonsectarian" prayer for public schools. ("Almighty God, we acknowledge our dependence upon Thee and we beg Thy blessings upon us, our parents, our teachers, and our country.") The Synagogue Council and the NJCRAC, along with Jewish civic agencies, civil liberties groups, liberal Protestant organizations, and individual dissenters, joined in briefs to the Supreme Court challenging these practices. In rapid-fire order, the Court handed down decisions banning the Regents' prayer (*Engel* v. *Vitale,* 1962), Bible-reading in public schools (*Abington Township* v. *Schempp,* 1963), prayer in public schools, and most forms of government financial assistance to private and parochial education.

A number of anomalies, however, were beginning to appear in the Jewish posture. As a result of postwar affluence and the building of the suburbs, Jews were leaving the cities in great numbers. Their children increasingly attended private schools or suburban public schools which, by virtue of their distance from urban problems, were, in effect, private schools operated at public expense. Meanwhile, however, Jewish organizations were arguing that it was necessary to maintain and strengthen the public schools in the cities because they were the single most important unifying force in society.

The irony, however, went deeper. In seeking to reduce the presence of religion in public institutions, Jews were helping to reduce its presence in American life as well. In striving to separate church and state, Jewish organizations earnestly believed that they were preventing religious harassment and providing safeguards for Jews, religious dissenters, and nonbelievers. A number of individuals and, of course, religious bodies were supporters of religion, but the activities of the organizations reflected the strong secular strain within Jewish life that was at best indifferent, when it was not actively hostile, to religion itself. Jewish organizations chose not to see that the "church" they sought to "disestablish" was not a sect but a collection of beliefs and values deeply embedded in society, values which, while causing uneasiness in religious outsiders, provided an order and coherence that had made it possible for Jews (and others) not only to live comfortably together but indeed to prosper.[44]

Resurgence of Orthodoxy

Many studies of American Judaism in the years following World War II assumed that American Jews were well on their way to assimilation into society. These studies suggested that Jews were ready to break with their traditional religious past. The war, however, brought another wave of immigration composed of Chasidic (a Jewish sect) and other elements, as well as several major rabbinic figures from Lithuania, which had been incorporated into the Soviet Union. Opposed to what they felt was the liberalism and social permissiveness of Orthodox "modernists," these rabbis encouraged in their students a style of life more like that of nineteenth-century Vilna than twentieth-century New York. Simultaneously, a revival of Orthodoxy was under way among young American-born and American-oriented Jews from Boston to Los Angeles. The militancy of these young people and Yeshiva students increasingly became a factor in Jewish life. Before long, the Orthodox group Agudath Israel established a new program called *Rishum* to get members of the organization more involved in Jewish concerns. Many of them, and those within Young Israel, were gradually politicized by such issues as the survival of Israel, the plight of Soviet Jewry, street crime against Jews, and the plight of the Jewish poor. These militant "new Jews" possessed values and attitudes that were at sharp variance with those of many of their coreligionists.[45] Hundreds of Jewish day schools and dozens of Yeshivas were founded, and attracted thousands who sought to identify with Orthodoxy. (In 1945 there were 78 Jewish day schools. By 1983 there were 540, with about 110,000 students.)[46] Many of the students came from poor or lower middle-class backgrounds.

Even Conservative Judaism, which was creating its own school system, felt new pressures. At the 1956 conference of the Rabbinical Assembly, a spirited debate broke out over a paper delivered by Rabbi Bernard Mandelbaum, who called for a new look at the "separation of church and state." When religion was eliminated from the school curriculum, he argued, a negative and distorted attitude toward it was encouraged. What was needed, he said, was to define more clearly what was genuine and necessary separation, as well as what form of cooperation was permissible and possibly even desirable. Mandelbaum was strongly challenged by Rabbi Morris Adler and others, who argued that any impairment of the principle of separation would open the door to broader dangers.

Although the Rabbinical Assembly voted in 1961 to "continue to oppose federal aid and loans to non-public schools," the broad consensus within American Jewry on the subject was beginning to be breached. During the same year, and for the first time, representatives of Agudath Israel told a House subcommittee in Washington that private schools had a right to benefit from government aid. To pay for their network of elementary and secondary schools with a total annual budget of $10 million, Agudath Israel argued, committed Orthodox parents would be forced to make financial sacrifices in order to pursue their religious beliefs. This, it was claimed, was a denial of freedom of choice.[47] Conscious of what an important segment of its constituency was feeling, the Union of Orthodox Jewish Congregations abstained in 1962 from the negative position taken by the NJCRAC on a specific bill to provide federal aid to parochial schools.[48]

The decisions handed down by the Supreme Court were a turning point in church-state relations and marked the emergence of what would later be called the "social issue"—a growing concern about changing values in American life among broad segments of the population. Small-town, rural, and more conservative Protestant elements became increasingly disturbed at the banning of prayer and Bible-reading from the schools, and eventually were joined by Roman Catholic leaders. The late Cardinal Spellman of New York was particularly harsh in his condemnation of the Court's decision in the Regents' prayer case.

Some of this anger came to rest on Jewish groups. In September 1962, the Catholic journal *America* carried an editorial entitled "To Our Jewish Friends." It predicted that the attitude of certain Jewish leaders would cause incidents of hostility to Jews, and blamed leaders of the CCAR, UAHC, and American Jewish Congress for precipitating the conflict, singling out Pfeffer by name. "What will have been accomplished if our Jewish friends win all the legal immunities they seek, but thereby paint themselves into a corner of social and cultural alienation?" the publication asked. Jewish leaders were furious.[49]

The twin Jewish—and liberal—goals of resolving the problems of the disadvantaged and opposing violations of the "separation" principle caused a problem, however, when the Johnson administration threw its support behind federal aid to schools in the Elementary and Secondary Education Act of 1965. Here, the two goals appeared to be in collision. For years, federal aid to education had been stymied by a number of factors, including the determination of the Roman Catholic Church to block such aid unless it was also given to private and parochial schools. This time, liberals backing the legislation came up with a compromise to overcome such opposition. They proposed a "child benefit" theory by which such aid would be provided to impoverished or handicapped children, rather than to school systems as such.

The legislation was supported by the National Education Association, the American Federation of Teachers, the National Council of Churches, and the great majority of Protestant denominations, as well as by most liberal groups. In announcing its support, the *New Republic* declared that "no useful purpose is served if [parochial school] children grow up knowing less history or less chemistry than children who attend public school. Ignorance, not the Catholic hierarchy, is the enemy."[50]

Jewish civic agencies and religious bodies, however, opposed portions of the act which, in their view, violated the separation principle. Speaking on behalf of Reform Judaism's Commission on Social Action, Rabbi Richard G. Hirsch reiterated his organization's support of public education while arguing that the measure tended "to equate public and church schools . . . as equally entitled to public support," thereby encouraging the creation of separate parochial school systems and weakening the public schools.[51] For similar reasons, local federations of Jewish agencies across the country also announced their opposition.

The split between Orthodox Jews and other Jewish groups now widened. Rabbi Morris Sherer of Agudath Israel, who explained that he was seeking aid only for the "general studies programs of the schools" and not for religious education, argued that it had never been government policy to favor public schools over others. He suggested that parochial schools contributed to the enrichment of American democracy and educational excellence. The spiritual leader of the Lubavitz Chasidic Movement, Rabbi Menachem Schneerson, said that Jews should be so committed to strengthening Jewish education that they should be willing to accept money from any source, including the government. Asked by Senator Jennings Randolph to explain the American Jewish Congress's opposition to the bill, an official of the National Society for Hebrew Day Schools declared that "it does not represent the religious community." As the debate raged, Agudath Israel helped to form a new religious rights body, the National Jewish Commission on Law and Public Affairs, which was made up of a group of bright young attorneys who were prepared to take on the legal staffs of the American Jewish Congress and the American Jewish Committee on certain issues, even as they were prepared to support them on others, such as the rights of Sabbath observers.[52]

After the Elementary and Secondary Education Act became law, the American Jewish Congress announced that it would file suit to overturn it, while the NJCRAC sought to limit its effects by proposing safeguards and urging member agencies to initiate court tests in states where the child benefit theory might be used to provide free bus transportation and remedial reading classes for pupils at non-public schools.[53] The cooperation between public and private schools envisioned by the legislation outraged Reform Judaism. Rabbi Hirsch declared that they "can no more be considered partners than can church and state be partners."[54] Reform went beyond groups like the National Council of Churches and the Baptist Joint Committee on Public Affairs—no less strong supporters of the "separation" principle—who looked to shared-time arrangements with parochial schools as a constitutionally viable way of relieving some of the burdens of these schools while exposing parochial school children to broader contacts with other children.

The collision between Jewish Orthodoxy and the more liberal Jewish groups, Egon Mayer has written, "is a paradigmatic expression of the differences in attitudes toward extracommunal assistance. The early immigrants and their native-born off-spring took pride in being 'self-made.' The immigrants of the post-war era take pride in knowing how to 'work the system.' " During the Johnson years, the latter "learned to fight for their fair share" in a manner that was unusual "in the American Jewish experience."[55]

Despite the strains that were beginning to appear both within the Jewish community and between it and other groups, in the mid-1960s the future had never seemed brighter for Jews. They had moved up in American life and had found themselves increasingly at home with their neighbors. Their social goals and values—what Stephen D. Isaacs has called their "religio-cultural obsession with the equalitarian ideal"—had also taken firm root in the broader society.[56] Indeed, liberalism had been installed as the secular religion not only of Jews but of America itself. As Jews looked to the years ahead, they had every reason to face the future with confidence and hope.

CHAPTER THREE

An Age of Anxiety (1965-1980)

> *Now, with the rise of black militancy and separatism
> . . . the uncovering of the ugly scar of anti-Semitism
> among many of those we thought we were so nobly
> helping, with the "third world" forces which we
> thought were so romantic and progressive now aligning
> themselves with Arabs against Israel, we are in a state
> of bitterness. . . .*
> RABBI EDWARD M. GERSHFIELD at the convention of the
> Rabbinical Assembly, 1970

EVEN AS JEWS CELEBRATED the greater opportunities opening up to them and others, dark clouds were forming that would cast shadows on their optimism. Racial disorders broke out in Harlem and Philadelphia in 1964 and in subsequent years spread to Watts in Los Angeles, Newark, Detroit, and other urban centers, finally ending in an orgy of destruction in 1968 following the murder of Martin Luther King, Jr. The Kerner Commission, appointed by President Johnson to examine the causes of the rioting, reported persuasively on the explosive social and economic conditions that existed in black slums. The commission's analysis focused on the responsibility of the broader society. An underlying racism pervaded America, it declared, and the United States was "moving toward two societies, one black, one white—separate and unequal." The commission's report concluded with numerous recommendations on how to improve conditions in the slums.[1]

The Race Revolution

Jews recognized well enough the problems facing blacks, but the racial disorders affected them differently than other Americans. Along with many blacks whose homes and neighborhoods had been burned out, Jews had also been victims of the disorders. As the proprietors of numerous small stores and businesses in the devastated areas, many Jews saw their lives endangered and their lifework wiped out. Yet they received little sympathy. Instead, the finger of blame was often pointed at them. In the immediate aftermath of the riots, it was alleged that exploitative practices by Jewish merchants had helped to bring about black rage. This view, however, was subsequently challenged by a number of government and other studies.[2]

For the most part, anti-Semitism was not a factor in the riots. It was simply that Jews were in the path of the urban storm, and during this period American cities saw a sharp increase in crime that often spilled over to the suburbs. In Philadelphia alone between 1968 and 1972, one study reported, at least twenty-two Jewish merchants were killed during robberies, and twenty-seven were shot or beaten.[3]

There were other disturbing elements as well. New black leaders were emerging—men like H. "Rap" Brown, Eldridge Cleaver, and Malcolm X—who differed in social background and goals from earlier middle-class leaders like Dr. King. The new leaders had given up on, or had never sought, racial desegregation; instead, they raised the banners of Black Nationalism and Black Power. Jews could understand, and even sympathize with, affirmations of black racial identity, but appeals for Black Power took an ugly turn. Radical intellectuals like Franz Fanon, Leroy Jones, and Harold Cruse compared the black struggle in America's slums with the efforts of colored peoples throughout the world to free themselves from colonial oppressors. In this context, Israel came to be seen as an outpost of Western and American imperialism. King fought against this view and sought to maintain the black-Jewish alliance. Ten days before his murder, he came before the Rabbinical Assembly and told his listeners, "I see Israel, and never mind saying it, as one of the great outposts of democracy in the world, and a marvelous example of what can be done, how desert land almost can be transformed into an oasis of brotherhood and democracy. Peace for Israel means security, and security must be a reality."[4]

In one of several widely publicized episodes, a Student Non-violent Coordinating Committee (SNCC) newsletter printed a cartoon showing a hand marked with the Star of David and a dollar sign tightening a rope around Egyptian leader Gamal Abdel Nasser and Cassius Clay (later Muhammad Ali). A month later, black delegates at a convention of the New Left were successful in winning approval of a statement condemning "Zionist imperialism."

Most disturbing of all were the provocative anti-Semitic statements made by many black militants. In a confrontation between a Congress of Racial Equality (CORE) official and the Jewish president of a Mount Vernon, N.Y., parents' and taxpayers' group over school desegregation, the former told the audience, a number of whom were Jewish, "Hitler made a mistake when he didn't kill enough of you." Malcolm X declared that blacks were better off with a white racist like the sheriff of Selma than with Jewish liberals: the sheriff was a wolf, but Jewish liberals were foxes. With a wolf one at least knew where one stood. Increasingly, Jews and liberals were seen as part of the "white power structure" that oppressed blacks.[5]

The civil rights revolution had turned into a race revolution which was becoming increasingly worrisome to Jews. The National Jewish Community Relations Advisory Council (NJCRAC) Joint Program Plan began reporting on anti-white feelings among blacks, on black demands for quotas for jobs, and on how vandalism threatened Jewish store owners in black neighborhoods.[6] In a statement on June 18, 1969, the Synagogue Council of America said that "even in pursuit of desirable ends, violence does not contribute to the fashioning of a better society; violence only breeds more violence, and nourishes repression, not justice." The United Synagogue condemned "violence and lawlessness as a means to redress social evils" and denounced anti-Semitic slurs. Somewhat defensively, it added that it did not need to apologize for the past efforts of Jews in the fight for black equality.[7] And when the president of New York University defended the appointment of a black militant who had written an article charging Jewish teachers with "educationally castrating" black children, the Union of American Hebrew Congregations (UAHC) denounced it as a "tortured and outraged effort to deodorize the noxious anti-Semitism" of the article.[8]

Two other episodes in New York aroused the uneasiness that Jews were coming to feel. They were the firing of thirteen Jewish teachers in Brooklyn's Ocean Hill–Brownsville area in a struggle over community control of the schools, and an attempt to introduce low-cost public housing in a mostly Jewish neighborhood of Forest Hills in Queens. The firing of the teachers was followed by a teachers' strike that produced a welter of charges. In 1969 the ADL concluded that "raw, undisguised anti-Semitism is at a crisis level in New York City where, unchecked by public authority, it has been building for two years."[9]

Differences on strategy were also developing between blacks and Jews. Many Jews believed that the goal of the civil rights revolution should be to strip away the unfair and undemocratic limitations faced by minorities so that they could rise or fall on individual merit, like other Americans. Blacks, however, now brought forward demands for "reparations," racial balance in schools, and "fair shares"—the idea that jobs, as well as admission to universities and graduate schools, should be apportioned along racial or ethnic lines. Most Jews favored affirmative action programs to broaden minority involvement in society, but they balked at quotas and preferential treatment. With long memories of how quotas had been used to keep Jews out of universities and professional schools, they feared that the institutionalization of quotas was a dangerous tendency, both for Jews and for the broader society.

In the late sixties and early seventies the race revolution became a catalyst in the rise of other groups, particularly Indians, Chicanos, women, and homosexuals. A whole new series of life-styles came into being. Not since Prohibition had there been such a gap between the "stated norms of society and actual behavior," Morris Dickstein declared. While Susan Sontag described the "new sensibility" favorably as the redemption of the senses from the mind,[10] Peter Schrag criticized it as a "cultural prison break."[11] Jews, like other Americans, now found themselves confronted by far more complex issues.

The Jewish Response

In the face of these new and often disturbing developments, most Jewish civic and religious bodies sought to remain true to their liberal tradition. Reform Judaism in particular sought to co-opt and even emulate the counterculture.[12] "One of the reasons for the youth revolt, the hippie movement, and the 'flower children,'" Vorspan declared in a volume for sixth-graders, "is the plea for love instead of so much violence and brutality," even if this was done in "foolish ways."[13] With the exception of a number of Orthodox groups, Jews backed the Equal Rights Amendment and other items on the liberal agenda. (Even the Union of Orthodox Jewish Congregations had a consistent record of supporting measures to ease the plight of agricultural and mine workers, and the Orthodox Rabbinical Council said that ERA posed "no threat to the practice of Judaism in the United States.")[14] Most of all, Jews felt obligated to remain in the struggle for racial justice, regardless of what blacks did or did not do. This was a requirement growing out of the "prophetic injunction to do justice," the SCA insisted. "We . . . will not be disengaged from that struggle for liberal race relations measures," the NJCRAC declared in 1968, "because some Negroes are violent, or ungrateful, or anti-Semitic."[15] While reiterating its earlier condemnation of "violence and lawlessness and slurs against Jews," the United Synagogue renewed its appeal to its congregations to help "make the Negro in fact a full citizen of these United States." The Union of Orthodox Jewish Congregations urged "all Jews to resist the sterile reaction of the 'blacklash' and to continue to erase bigotry, intolerance and prejudice from their own business, professional, and personal lives. . . ."

Reform Judaism was especially active and outspoken. A 1968 message issued by the Committee on Justice and Peace of the Central Conference of American Rabbis (CCAR) called upon Jews "who are the merciful sons of merciful fathers to avoid siren calls to retire from the struggle and . . . [try] to understand both the rational and irrational aspects of Black Power." In *Jewish Values and Social Crisis: A Casebook on Social Action,* published by the UAHC, Vorspan sought to explain the new black militancy. "The riots in our cities are the flaming code language by which the Negro is trying to say: I can no longer wait for those rights and opportunities without which I cannot become a self-respecting man."[16] And in *Justice, Justice,* also published by the UAHC, Rabbi Henry Cohen wrote that "the popular impression that anti-Semitism is running rampant in the Negro communities provides many Jews with what they consider a justification for being indifferent to the Civil Rights movement." Rabbi Cohen cited an earlier analysis underwritten by the ADL to the effect that blacks were not anti-Semitic. But aware that the issue could not be ignored, he argued that blacks expressed their attitudes more openly than whites. There was so much frustration in the black community "that anti-Semitic Negroes may feel comparatively less inhibited about openly voicing and acting out their prejudices."[17]

The message of Jewish organizations to their members was that Jews should "see with our mind and hearts . . . [the] combination of conditions . . . [that] can produce the kind of frustration and despair that explodes into violence." They could then "transform the memory of Jewish suffering into compassion for the victims of racial injustice."

There were also Jews who had been trapped in the slums by history and social change, but remarkably little sympathy was expended on them, even by other Jews. Rabbi Harold Schulweiss suggested that if Jewish merchants had to charge high prices because of theft or high interest rates, they should leave the ghettos. Jews, he said, should not live off the misery of the poor.[18] But as Jewish businessmen were forced out or voluntarily departed, the ghettos became more depressed and barren than ever before.

Jewish groups now fell back on traditional formulas for eradicating the conditions that bred poverty and violence. In his *Casebook,* Vorspan called for the creation of two million jobs for the black unemployed. If private industry could not or would not provide them, it was the responsibility of government to do so. Only through the latter, the NJCRAC argued in 1965, "can objectives of an anti-poverty program be obtained." The following year the organization supported "fundamental and drastic changes in the economic . . . organization of our society to accomplish this," and Vorspan suggested that one way would be to cut the defense budget, which would be an "instance where one good deed drags in its wake another."[19] In 1968 the NJCRAC perceived a "danger" that too much reliance was being placed on private enterprise to reduce poverty. And although at least part of the problem was the large number of unskilled, undereducated, slum-shocked youths who needed to learn orderly work habits and be introduced to the world of employment, the NJCRAC in 1972 opposed the establishment of a bi-level minimum wage with a lower level for teenagers, a move that some believed would create more jobs in the ghettos.

Rising Crime

As crime became a matter of increasing concern to Americans in the late sixties, Jewish groups tended to see it as a symptom of a deeper malaise stemming from poverty, hopelessness, and discrimination. "People who feel trapped, helpless, and angry, and who feel they have no stake in their society, explode into violence very easily," said Vorspan.[20] Jewish groups also worried about the political consequences of crime, since some conservative and right-wing politicians were attacking liberals for "coddling" criminals.

The Jewish groups tended to focus on long-range social and economic ameliorative efforts. The Rabbinical Assembly urged Congress in 1968 to spend for the "domestic war" on poverty and all related evils in the city.[21] In its 1969 Joint Program Plan, the NJCRAC included a synopsis of the Kerner Commission recommendations and the AJCommittee, AJCongress, ADL, UAHC, United Synagogue, National Council of Jewish Women, and seventeen Christian groups jointly issued a pamphlet summarizing and advocating the broad social programs advocated by the Kerner Commission.[22] There was even some disposition to see certain positive results stemming from the rioting. "Behavior, even shocking, seemingly pathological behavior, has meaning," Dean Alex Rosen of the New York University Graduate School of Social Work wrote in the foreword to an American Jewish Committee study of the Philadelphia rioting. He noted that "group violence, of which a race riot is one example, . . . is a form of inarticulate language in which one group of people *communicates* with other groups about its feelings, its problems, its life circumstances. . . ."[23]

As for punishing crime, Vorspan told his sixth-grade Jewish readers, "violence only breeds more violence." Did not executing murderers, he asked them, make "matters worse by making the state—and, therefore, all the people—legal murderers? Shouldn't we try to save the person who has committed crimes, even the bloodiest crimes, instead of killing him?" He found that punishment, even for those sentenced for violent crime, did not usually improve a person or make him fit for decent life in a civilized society. It made him become all the more bitter and "want to punish society back."[24]

Although the American Jewish Committee, along with the Urban League and other groups, sparked a Safer Cities program aimed at broader citizen involvement in the battle against crime, there was little attention to the plight of victims and only the most modest effort to address the "here and now" aspects of the problem. The NJCRAC and other Jewish organizations did support a program of government loans for blacks who wanted to buy Jewish-owned stores in the ghettos, and in a few cities a small number of such exchanges occurred. Jewish agencies also pressed for greater police effort against criminal violence and sought the licensing of handguns. But their main emphasis was on blaming society for crime and reducing police abuses. The NJCRAC in 1970 called for the establishment of civilian review boards, special councils for the protection of civil liberties, the reform of police courts, and the creation of social programs "in preference to the acquisition of police armaments." There was little recognition of the legitimate and growing concern about crime and about the victims of crime that was being expressed at all levels of society.

The Jewish Left

While established Jewish groups offered a generalized liberal response to racial issues, a radical Jewish culture still survived the loss of Communist effectiveness largely centered in New York. Several of the new black militants like Stokely Carmichael on the East Coast and Ron Karenga on the West Coast had been heavily affected by it in developing their philosophy and protest and propaganda techniques, the former through contact with Jews he met at the Bronx High School of Science. What historical scholarship has demonstrated most recently is the important role played by Jewish radical thought in helping to shape the black radical movement of the latter part of the 1960s. Carmichael particularly reflected this Afro-American/Jewish radicalism in his verbal attacks on the hypocrisy of conventional liberalism and middle class values.[25]

As radical ferment swept across American life in the late 1960s and early 1970s, Jewish students were at the forefront of change. Arthur Liebman has said that the membership of Students for a Democratic

Society (SDS) was somewhere between 30 and 50 per cent Jewish. Most of the members of the Free Speech Movement in Berkeley in 1964 were Jews.[26] Earlier, it had been suggested that there was little in the initial Jewish youth revolt that was identifiably Jewish. By the late 1960s, however, a number of "New Jews" in groups like Jews for Urban Justice and the Jewish Liberation Project were seeking to find in Jewish tradition a rationale for their "commitment . . . and participation in revolutionary struggles."[27] Among them was Arthur I. Waskow, an alternate delegate to the tumultuous 1968 Democratic National Convention in Chicago and a founder of the Institute for Policy Studies, a left-wing organization in Washington.

Waskow called the 1968 rioting in the District of Columbia "the April uprising of Black Washington against the blank-eyed pyramid-builders of our time. . . ." He compared the burned-out stores of Washington, "emptied of food and watches," to what had happened centuries earlier, "when the Israelites looted Egypt of gold and jewels before they left, as reparations for four centuries of slavery." With several friends, Waskow wrote a Freedom Seder. Published in *Ramparts* magazine and then as a book, Waskow's Seder received considerable attention in certain Jewish youth and radical circles. It made explicit for a contemporary audience the theme of the original Seder, the ancient struggle of the Jewish people for freedom. Waskow wove quotations from Jefferson, Thoreau, Buber, Eldridge Cleaver, and the Berrigan brothers into his Seder, and juxtaposed the uprising of the Jews in the Warsaw ghetto with the rioting in American ghettos as part of the same "liberationist struggle."[28]

While Waskow brilliantly exploited a rich Jewish theme, he ignored the criminal violence against small-scale Jewish merchants in the slums. Moreover, the looting of liquor stores was hardly the moral equivalent of blacks in the South facing cattle prods for trying to vote, or Jews rising up against the Nazis. Morally appealing as certain aspects of the Jewish radical movement in the sixties may have been, the movement was also the ultimate expression of the Jewish utopian temperament. It was almost completely decoupled from reality.

School Desegregation

Even as the more militant black leadership moved away from efforts to achieve desegregation in favor of black economic and political power, most Jewish groups continued their strong support for racial integration. Since most of the legal barriers to integration were down or were coming down, the fight shifted to efforts to achieve some form of racial balance in schools losing white students, particularly schools in the urban centers of the Northeast and West. The NJCRAC argued in 1965 that "racial integration is an essential component of good education," adding that "a black child's stigma is the same whether his segregation is enforced by law or custom or merely circumstances." Such a black child is inherently "impaired in his motivation and his ability to learn." Four years later the NJCRAC endorsed community control of schools but added that "this must be reconciled with the values of effectiveness and efficiency." In the early 1970s the organization endorsed a series of government actions to enforce desegregation, including denying or granting federal funds to local school districts on the basis of their efforts to achieve integration, improving inner city schools to eliminate the disparities between them and suburban schools, changing school district lines and feeder patterns, and busing students to other schools.

By the latter part of the 1970s the Union of Orthodox Jewish Congregations and the American Jewish Committee, which supported desegregation, were abstaining from similar declarations by the NJCRAC, largely because of the busing issue.[29] In effect, the NJCRAC continued to argue that unless blacks sat next to whites, even when official segregation no longer existed, the former would be educationally and socially harmed. There was some validity, of course, to the view that "black schools" were often poorer schools with less experienced teachers and fewer physical resources. As black pride grew, some blacks began to suggest that the schools in their neighborhoods should be improved, and that black children should not be forced to travel to other, often hostile, environments.

Racial Quotas

It was on the matter of racial quotas that Jews had their sharpest conflicts with black leaders. Although most Jews saw quotas as anathema, the NJCRAC as early as 1964, they had customarily supported affirmative action programs. In 1971 the organization urged that "major priority" be given such efforts, and this view was endorsed by the Synagogue Council a year later.[30] But the 1971 NJCRAC statement called for specific goals and timetables in affirmative action programs, and some argued that these would lead inevitably to racial quotas. The critics of the NJCRAC felt that "advancement in employment must be based on merit alone" and agreed with Morris B. Abram, former president of the American Jewish Committee, that an emphasis on preferential treatment based on racial distinctions had corroded the body politic.

The conflict between Jews and blacks came to a head in two legal cases, one involving a white denied admission to a law school (*De Funis* v. *Odegard*, 1974), the other involving a white denied admission to a medical school (*Bakke* v. *University of California*, 1978). Both schools had quotas for minorities. The strong anti-quota stand taken by most Jewish groups in their briefs before the Supreme Court on behalf of the white candidates brought them into collision with black leaders as well as with liberal and civil liberties groups.

Welfare Reform

During the Nixon years (1969-1974), Jewish groups struggled to sustain the philosophies that had guided them for so long. The NJCRAC expressed general disapproval of Nixon's social policies, particularly cuts in federal domestic spending. In reaffirming its 1966 position paper, "Next Steps in the Fight for Equality," the organization noted that the president had curtailed low-cost housing and taken steps that increased unemployment among the poor. Similarly, the Conference of Jewish Communal Service and the Synagogue Council of America called for improvements in the anti-poverty laws and expanded job opportunities for the disadvantaged.[31] The United Synagogue of America called for a "federally funded and administered program that would ultimately replace the present welfare system."

When the Nixon administration surprised everyone by proposing a Family Assistance Program (FAP) that would provide the poor, including the working poor, with a minimum income, Jewish groups were not sure how to respond. During the next two years the proposal was caught between liberals who felt the minimum was too low and conservatives who believed the program would open the door to further "socialist" moves. In April 1970 the House of Representatives approved the legislation by a large majority, and the bill then moved to the Senate. There, during hearings before the Senate Finance Committee, Hyman Bookbinder of the American Jewish Committee urged the senators and his fellow liberals not to let "the best be the enemy of the good." The Synagogue Council of America joined the major Protestant and Catholic organizations in supporting the bill.

But the religious organizations gradually found the legislation to be less liberal than they wished. They recommended an increase in the minimum income that the legislation would provide for families, and coverage of single persons and childless couples; they also called the legislation's proposed work requirements for those who would benefit from the law "arbitrary and unnatural." These demands severely damaged the legislation's chances. The best had indeed become the enemy of the good, and the bill died in the Senate.[32]

Class Conflict

It was becoming apparent by the early seventies that opposition to the liberal policies supported by many Jewish organizations was rising within the Jewish community. Poorer and less educated Jews, many of them Orthodox, as well as Jewish small businessmen and Jews in the lower and middle ranks of the civil service—those, in short, directly affected by the urban crisis—were the most restless. They felt that their more affluent brethren were more distant from urban problems and therefore had less to lose. Liberal politicians like New York mayor John Lindsay and Democratic presidential candidate George McGovern worried them. These middle-rank Jews were joined by intellectuals like Earl Raab, Milton Himmelfarb, and Maurice Goldbloom, who argued that liberal Protestant and other upper-class elites were willing to purchase social peace by, in effect, selling out the Jews.[33]

More and more, the annual Joint Program Plan of the NJCRAC was pockmarked by dissents and abstentions. When the NJCRAC reaffirmed its approval of busing for school desegregation in the 1974-75 plan, for instance, the UOJC abstained. The UOJC, the ADL, and several local community relations councils objected to a section of the plan that urged special consideration for the disadvantaged by employers and university admissions officials. They argued that NJCRAC policy was to oppose both discrimination and reverse discrimination, and to support individual merit.[34] When the NJCRAC reaffirmed its opposition to capital punishment, the Jewish Labor Committee and the UOJC abstained. When the NJCRAC urged other agencies to "engage actively in programs and public interpretation stressing the importance of scrupulous protections of individual freedoms" of those accused of crime, the ADL found this too broad, and the UOJC abstained.[35] With obvious reference to the question of introducing low-cost public housing in Forest Hills, the ADL and the UOJC proposed that the plan recognize "the desirability of maintaining the homogeneity of religious communities within the broader context of integrated housing."[36] While it "unequivocally" championed equal rights for women, the UOJC continued its opposition to the proposed Equal Rights Amendment.[37] As it had done since the mid-1960s, the UOJC dissented from opposition to federal aid for parochial schools, seeing such opposition as "serving to support imposition of a monolithic secular direction on American education, society, and life."[38]

Clearly, important segments of the Jewish community were turning inward and seeking greater self-protection. One indication of this was the formation of the Jewish Defense League (JDL) following the New York City teacher strike in 1968. Led by an Orthodox rabbi, Meir Kahane, the JDL's base was largely among Orthodox elements and lower middle-class Jews. Its vigilante tactics were condemned by practically all segments of the organized Jewish community. The president of the UAHC, for example, charged that "Jews carrying baseball bats and chains, standing in phalanxes like goon squads in front of synagogues, led by rabbis, are no less offensive and, in essence, no different from whites carrying robes and hood, led by self-styled ministers of the gospel, standing in front of burning crosses."[39] But despite the JDL's small numbers and objectionable tactics, its motto "Never Again" caught the mood that was developing among many Jews.

Other and more respected Jewish leaders also began to raise questions about the traditional liberalism of Jews. Rabbi Seymour Siegel of the Jewish Theological Seminary in New York wrote a scathing attack on liberalism in a 1972 issue of *Judaism*. "It is my belief that as Americans and as Jews, we have arrived at the time for a change." Noting that liberalism had "performed yeoman service in the four decades during which" it was the dominant force in American politics, Siegel now found it "inimical to Jewish interests" and not reflective of the "basic tenets of the Jewish tradition." He was joined by Rabbi Wolfe Kelman, executive vice president of the Rabbinical Assembly, who had been a close associate of Rabbi Heschel's. Following the uproar over public housing in Forest Hills, the two men formed the Jewish Rights Council. Jews must deal with broader community problems, Kelman explained, but they must also ask, "what's good for Jews?"[40]

Rabbi Arthur Hertzberg, on the other hand, tried to infuse the older liberal tradition with a new realism. As early as 1964, Hertzberg had recognized that Jewish organizations that took civil rights battles as "their sole contemporary reason for being" were engaged in "institutional suicide" and should deal more with "the question of their own spiritual and cultural survival in America [and] concern for the rest of world Jewry."[41] In a speech before the NJCRAC in 1973, he warned that the Jewish "establishment" was no longer attuned to the problems of the Jewish poor: "We are not really speaking for a Jewish community anymore, as perhaps we could in an earlier time when we could sing 'We Shall Overcome' and then fly back to our quasi-public schools in Tenafly or Scarsdale." Despite this, he argued, Jews could not ignore the country's twenty million blacks. "If we keep tinkering with the society, keep bringing more resources to play, keep putting more people together, keep bringing more elements within the society forward, then perhaps we can escape the explosion."[42]

Israel

One element that unified the entire Jewish community was the Six-Day War between Israel and surrounding Arab countries in June 1967. For a brief period, as Egypt reported its armies sweeping toward the sea, it seemed as if another Holocaust was in the offing. But the Israeli victories both in the 1967 conflict and in the Yom Kippur War in 1973 marked a turning point for Jews. Events had combined to challenge the basic premises of the liberalism and rationalism that underlay the public policy formulations of American Jews. The world, it was increasingly seen, was a dangerous place where orderly progress based on good will and on close association with allies, white and black, was far from automatic. Armed strength mattered more than rhetoric about peace, justice, and good will. It was no coincidence that almost a generation passed after World War II before American Jews were able to come to grips with the Holocaust. In consequence, growing numbers of them began to see powerlessness as the greatest evil. American Jews would continue to vote as liberals, but the center of their attention moved elsewhere. Israel had become, in effect, the religion of American Jews, Nathan Glazer declared in the epilogue of *American Judaism* in 1972, and "ethnic loyalty . . . ever more paramount as the significant content of Judaism."

Jewish concern about Israel brought into question the role of the United Nations. In the late sixties, that organization came to be dominated by Arab and Third World countries, often backed by the Soviet Union and its satellites. As a majority of the U.N. General Assembly became more hostile to Israel, Jewish groups became more critical of many U.N. activities. In 1970 the NJCRAC attacked the world body "for adopting resolutions critical of Israel and not of Arab states."[43] Following the roaring welcome given PLO leader Yasser Arafat when he visited the United Nations headquarters in 1975, the United Synagogue declared that "the U.N. has come perilously close to complete moral and ethical bankruptcy and its resolutions must be seen as a reflection of . . . essentially anti-democratic, anti-Western, and anti-Semitic hatreds."

The 1975 U.N. resolution stating that Zionism was a form of racism was the crowning blow. The resolution sought to deny Jews what the United Nations at least in principle accorded every other people—the right to control their own destiny in a sovereign state. Jewish groups now urged the United States to limit its commitment to the world organization. The Rabbinical Assembly called on "the world community in general and the United States in particular to withhold support for efforts to introduce the concept into U.N. programs and activities."

The NJCRAC proposed that the United States "work outside the U.N. if the situation warrants" and that American assistance to U.N. programs be tied to the voting records of countries that were recipients of assistance under those programs.[44]

Viet Nam

Like most Americans, Jews were torn by the debate over U.S. involvement in Viet Nam. The representative bodies were, of course, strongly opposed to the Soviet Union and the spread of Communism. However, Jewish tradition also stood firmly against "militarism" and war. There was still some resonance in the view taken by the Rabbinical Assembly in 1934 that no war is a righteous war, that idealistic "objectives . . . have generally been a camouflage for economic imperialism." The Jewish suspicion of militarism could also be seen in a CCAR resolution adopted shortly after World War II that called for democratizing the armed forces by abolishing all distinctions between officers and enlisted personnel.[45] Jewish groups were also deeply worried about the possibility of a nuclear conflagration growing out of a limited war.

It is difficult now to understand why U.S. involvement in Viet Nam drew so little attention for a decade. That inattention ended only in 1965, when President Johnson committed American troops to combat and authorized limited bombing of North Viet Nam. The initial response of most Jewish groups to the president's actions was relatively mild. In January 1966 the Synagogue Council announced that for "the first time . . . the entire Jewish religious community had taken a position on an international issue going beyond immediate Jewish concern." The council commended President Johnson for temporarily halting the bombing and called for negotiations on a cease-fire agreement "including representation for the National Liberation Front and other interested parties." The UAHC heard Rabbi Eisendrath warn that American policy bore "all the stigmata of the white man's imperialism," but it adopted a compromise resolution calling for negotiations to end the conflict.[46] With the exception of the American Jewish Congress, Jewish civic agencies felt it was not within their purview to take a position on the war.[47]

The moderate tone of the early response is best caught in the January 1966 Synagogue Council resolution:

> We do not lay claim to moral certitude and refrain from moral dogmatism in this complex and agonizing situation. Within the range of religious commitment and concern, differences as to specific policies can and do exist. We recognize that those who see the need for checking Communist subversion by military means are no less dedicated to the cause of a just world peace than those who believe the United States must cease hostilities in Viet Nam. We do believe, however, that the imperatives of our religious commitments call for the recommendations we prayerfully put forward and commend to the attention of our synagogues throughout the land.

52   THE UTOPIAN DILEMMA

The following year the United Synagogue was convinced of the need for "continued patience." But the Jewish War Veterans of the U.S.A. were joined in their support of the war by the Union of Orthodox Jewish Congregations, which passed a resolution supporting U.S. determination to resist Communist aggression anywhere in the world.[48]

Increasingly, however, the temper of the debate escalated. In several instances, extreme elements engaged in sabotage and violence to protest the larger violence practiced by the United States in Viet Nam. Much of the passion that had animated the civil rights movement shifted to protesting the war. In April 1967, Martin Luther King delivered a major anti-war address attacking U.S. involvement in Viet Nam in New York's Riverside Church. Rabbi Heschel was among the other speakers.[49] On the day after 400,000 anti-war demonstrators marched in Washington, groups associated with Jews for Urban Justice gathered to pray. They debated the war, destroyed representations of the Golden Calf, and sounded the Shofar. Later, the Jewish radical resistance movement sponsored Freedom Seders around the country. At one of these, at Cornell University in 1970, the door was opened symbolically for the arrival of the prophet Elijah. The person who appeared instead was the Catholic priest Daniel Berrigan, then in hiding for illegal anti-war activity.[50]

Enormous pressure was placed on the Jewish community from all directions. At a meeting with Jewish war veterans, President Johnson compared the U.S. commitment to South Viet Nam with its commitment to Israel. He seemed to suggest that American support for Israel would depend on Jewish backing for the U.S. position in Viet Nam, but when the substance of this meeting was reported in the press, the White House denied any connection.[51] Later, during the Nixon presidency, representatives of the Israeli government visited American Jewish leaders, including Rabbi Heschel and Rabbi Balfour Brickner, to urge them to end their public protests against the war. (Heschel, according to Brickner, was "beside himself with grief and anger" at this intervention.[52])

Despite the gradual withdrawal of American troops from Viet Nam in 1969 and 1970, opposition to the war increased within the Jewish community. This opposition probably reached its high point during the 1969 Moratorium Day, when the CCAR, the UAHC, Hadassah, Labor

Zionists, and the Synagogue Council, among others, issued statements calling for an end to the war and affirming the right to dissent from government policy. The ADL flew its flag at half-mast. Jewish groups saw a clear distinction between their opposition to the war in Viet Nam and their support for Israel during its 1967 war with its Arab neighbors. "What choice did they have when the latter sought to destroy Israel and drive its people into the sea?" Vorspan asked.[53]

When the Nixon administration began an offensive in the spring of 1970 against Communist sanctuaries in Cambodia and resumed the bombing of North Viet Nam, most of the Jewish civic agencies and religious bodies were highly critical. But some, including Agudath Israel, backed Nixon's "intensive effort to achieve an honorable peace." Reform Judaism was more militant than other Jewish groups in its criticism of the administration. In a 1972 resolution, the CCAR said that it "completely disassociates itself from the immoral actions perpetrated by the government of the United States" and called for "national atonement."

A central issue for Jewish groups was the nature of dissent and its limits. Generally, they favored greater latitude for dissent. In 1968 the CCAR adopted a resolution that commended all those who "acting out of commitment to the prophetic ideals of justice and peace . . . conscientiously dissent from the policy of our government in Viet Nam and who refuse to cooperate with that policy." At one point the CCAR urged members of the Hebrew Union College–Jewish Institute of Religion and UAHC to withhold payment of the telephone excise tax as an expression of opposition to the war. And when six rabbis were arrested at the John F. Kennedy Federal Building in Boston while participating in an act of nonviolent civil disobedience, the CCAR applauded them.[54]

Throughout the war, a majority of the Jewish groups called for a broadening of the definition of conscientious objector. The Rabbinical Assembly argued for "selective conscientious objection"—extending the concept to objection to a particular war—as grounds for exemption from military service. The UAHC adopted the same position a year later. On the other hand, the Rabbinical Council (an Orthodox group) condemned the burning of draft cards as a "clear violation of the basic process of democracy."[55] After the war ended, Jewish groups had different ideas about the various forms of amnesty proposed by Presidents Ford and Carter for those who had refused to serve in the armed forces.

Whatever one's views on the merits of U.S. involvement in Viet Nam, it is clear that major mistakes were made in defining U.S. objectives and selecting the most appropriate ways of achieving them. Once the United States was involved, however, a complex dynamic was set in motion involving America's obligations as a world power. On the whole, there seems to have been little recognition of this among Jewish groups, which led to a lack of realism in much of the Jewish response to the war.

Negotiation was, for North Viet Nam, an adjunct of violence. By placing so much unilateral pressure on the U.S. government, Jewish (and other religious and secular groups) weakened the capacity of the president to bring about a stable and just peace. The nature of the Hanoi regime came into sharper focus later in the 1970s with its invasion of Cambodia, expulsion of ethnic Chinese, and establishment of a system of "re-education" camps. Jewish groups did not glorify the Viet Cong or North Viet Nam, as some of the more radical anti-war elements did, but they exhibited little patience with the Saigon regime. While not conforming to our standard of democracy, South Viet Nam had at least the potentiality for developing free institutions. The positions of many Jewish groups ultimately came to reflect what Rabbi Richard Rubinstein has called the "liberal illusion that . . . the voice of moderation can usually triumph."[56]

An Age of Anxiety

The Golden Age of American Jewry was over before Jews had a chance to enjoy it fully. By the 1970s there was no mistaking the new sense of anxiety felt by Jews. Noting the assassinations of John F. Kennedy, Robert Kennedy, and Martin Luther King, and the race riots in the cities, Vorspan asked, "What is wrong with America that leads to such dreadful violence?" A report of the National Opinion Research Center on the "levels of distrust" among white ethnic groups found the level of distrust among Jews almost leaping off the chart.[57] As Jews encountered new pressures both within and outside the Jewish community, the moral anguish of the Jewish leadership became acute.

The conflict felt by Jews was played out in a famous symposium, "Liberalism and the Jews," in the January 1980 issue of *Commentary*. There fifty-two Jewish leaders debated the relevance of liberalism, in its current setting, to the concerns of Jews. "I have not changed my views on human equality or freedom one whit," wrote Morris B. Abram, the former head of the American Jewish Committee who had led the fight that resulted in the Supreme Court's one-man, one-vote decision. The endorsement of racial quotas was nothing less "than a demand that government should classify and treat Americans on a basis which liberals had denounced for one hundred years as contemptible and invidious." "I have been chastened in my hopes that government can produce greater social justice," wrote Eugene B. Borowitz, editor of the journal *Sh'ma,* only to add a few sentences later, "I and other Jews remain liberal because we fear the undemocratic forces on the Right more than big government or anything we see on the Left."

This debate had broken out with special force earlier at a convention of the Rabbinical Assembly, in numbers and philosophy perhaps the most reflective of American Jewry as a whole. Rabbi Edward M. Gershfield declared that Conservative Judaism was a "centrist movement," but that philosophically and socially "we are living in an age of extremes." Conservative Judaism had been built on reason, but the "unthinking regimentation and emotionalism" of Orthodoxy "had become more attractive." Jewish youth wanted "excitement and noise, improvisation and emotion . . . informality and spontaneity." Rabbi Gershfield noted that the steam had gone out of the civil rights movement, and that Jews were confused. "Now, with the rise of black militancy and separatism . . . the uncovering of the ugly scar of anti-Semitism among many of those we thought we were so nobly helping, with the 'third world' forces which we thought were so romantic and progressive now aligning themselves with Arabs against Israel, we are in a state of bitterness. . . ." Vietnam, he declared, had caused "an outpouring of pilpul [casuistry] to show that our dovishness . . . did not preclude . . . favoring American intervention on behalf of Israel."

Rabbi Gershfield was followed to the podium by Rabbi Mayer Abramowitz, who said that the Jewish community would have been better served if rabbis and laymen had exerted their energies more on behalf of Jews. "In demonstrating for peace, a noble and just cause beyond any doubt, we have contributed toward destroying the image of

Israel." By branding the United States as the aggressor, Jews had not challenged those who had marched with the banner of the Viet Cong: ". . . it is we, American rabbis, who have helped to tarnish . . . [Israel's] image by contributing to the respectability of Russia—by being mute to the cry of violence within its borders and to its shipment of war beyond its borders." Abramowitz closed with a recommendation: "It is for these reasons that I turn to my colleagues with the proposition that we should withdraw from active liberalism."[58]

After another rabbi declared that this was the first convention where the JDL view had been heard, Rabbi Morris Margolis urged his audience not to turn its back on the suffering of others, an indifference which had once led to the crematoria. It was not possible to talk about the "Negro problem," or anyone else's. It is one world, he said. "There will be no American Judaism," he concluded, "if . . . we refuse to fight for what is right simply because there are people . . . who don't appreciate what we are doing for them . . . . We are doing it for us."[59]

The debate caught with unusual poignancy the dilemma facing Jews, who only a few years before had "assumed that progress toward a new and better order of things was possible."[60] Even Reform Judaism, whose view was that the Jewish religious tradition should inform the reordering of society, was caught up in this new soberness. While expressing pleasure at how much of its "pioneering conception of Judaism had been accepted by the Household of Israel," its "Centenary Perspective" in 1976 noted that until recently "our obligations to the Jewish people and to all humanity seemed congruent." Now, it found, "these two imperatives appear to conflict." The "Centenary Perspective" reported that Reform Judaism knew no way to resolve this conflict other than to confront it "without abandoning either of our commitments."[61]

Meanwhile, Rabbi Heschel, the leading religious figure of the Golden Age, had been forced to the sidelines. His last work was published in 1973, a year after his death. Its subject, the Kotzker Rebbe, showed that Heschel had again turned inward. He did so, Hillel Goldberg has suggested, not because of the self-indulgence so characteristic of the period, but to find out what had gone wrong.[62]

CHAPTER FOUR

New Stirrings (1975-1984)

The era of liberal internationalism, extending from World War I until 1980, has pretty much petered out. The old liberal establishment . . . has lost, to a large degree, its credibility, its authority, and its political influence.
IRVING KRISTOL[1]

THE LATE SEVENTIES saw the exacerbation of trends that had concerned many Americans for some time. There was growing restlessness about the steep growth in governmental spending and the tax increases necessary to pay for it. Many saw their taxes as being used to support a seemingly permanent welfare class. Although Americans had shown a willingness to underwrite programs for helping those in dire economic straits through no fault of their own, the problems of minorities in the inner cities seemed to be growing worse.

Many were also worried about personal violence—rape, robbery, assault, murder. "The chance of being a victim of a violent crime," Charles Silberman wrote, "nearly tripled between 1960 and 1976. . . ."[2] To many, the growth in violence seemed linked to a greater degree of permissiveness and a breakdown in community standards. They saw this breakdown as responsible for the soaring number of teen-age abortions, the proliferation of X-rated films, and heavy emphasis in television on violence and extramarital sex. They were offended as well by the argument that homosexuality was simply an alternative life-style, and they were concerned about the rapid spread of the drug culture.

New Ideological and Political Stirrings

Considerable numbers of Americans found themselves disturbed as well by the erosion of American power and influence in the world. Two events in the closing months of the Carter administration highlighted the U.S. decline. The first was the Soviet invasion of Afghanistan despite vehement U.S. protests and a subsequent embargo on the shipment of U.S. grain to the Soviet Union. The second was the assault on the U.S. Embassy in Teheran by Iranian zealots and the seizure of Americans there as hostages. As the months wore on and negotiations failed to secure the release of the hostages, it was brought home to many that the government seemed incapable of summoning up the will to protect itself and its citizens. A new, nationalistic mood began to develop.

One result of these events was the growth of the New Right, which sought a strengthening of U.S. military might, tougher action against criminals (including restoration of the death penalty), the return of Bible-reading and prayer in public schools, and reversal of the 1973 Supreme Court decision that legalized abortion. Other targets of the New Right were the busing of school children to achieve integration, racial quotas, and the Equal Rights Amendment. The Moral Majority and the Coalition for Better Television sought to ban certain books in the public schools and to influence television shows they deemed morally offensive.

The election of Ronald Reagan in 1980 brought many of these ideas to the fore. In line with his own ideological conservatism and the promptings of the right-wing constituency that had helped elect him, Reagan moved to strengthen the U.S. military posture and slow the growth of the welfare state. He also threw his support behind a number of positions on public policy issues endorsed by the New Right.

Meanwhile, a new body of social criticism not easily catalogued as coming from the Left or the Right gained prominence and respectability in American life. One subject of particular interest to the new critics was the nature of poverty and what role government should play in trying to mitigate it. Blanche Bernstein, former commissioner of New York City's Human Resources Commission, and writer Ken Auletta reported that the number of Americans on welfare expanded from 2.2

million in 1950 to 10.4 million in 1979 despite generally good economic conditions and the elimination of legalized discrimination.

Some of this growth in welfare was due to greater recognition of society's obligations to the poor, structural changes in the economy, and the economic downturns of the 1970s. Observers of social welfare programs said that this growth was also due to the "feminization of poverty." In 1980 the U.S. Census Bureau reported that 41 per cent of black families were headed by women without husbands, an increase of a third within ten years. Black children living in one-parent homes, it was estimated, accounted for 80 per cent of the black poor.[3] This was a new and different kind of poverty than that experienced during the Great Depression.

The new critics argued that welfare benefits had hurt as well as helped poor people because they led to dependency. Since "the poor and welfare remain substantial abstractions," Auletta charged, "many otherwise intelligent people are as ignorant of the true plight of the poor as they correctly accuse Ronald Reagan of being." Auletta called for a mix of strategies—"liberal compassion" coupled with "conservative toughness." Others challenged the widespread assumption that poverty and poverty-related programs were primarily responsible for the growth in government expenditures. The fact was that over the decades a number of entitlement programs had been created that were aimed largely at the middle class; some, of course, helped those at the bottom of the scale as well. Moreover, the large constituencies that benefited from these programs made any cutbacks close to impossible politically. The irony here was that minorities and the poor were not the major beneficiaries of the welfare state.[4]

As disenchantment with government programs increased, greater attention began to be paid to informal and age-old modes of dealing with social problems. In a seminal analysis in 1977, Peter Berger and Richard Neuhaus noted that "mediating structures" like families, neighborhoods, churches, and ethnic groups had been the primary instruments for coping with problems before the rise of the welfare state. The creation of vast impersonal government bureaucracies, while useful and even necessary at the time, had weakened the functioning of these traditional institutions. Berger and Neuhaus called for an exploration of ways to help reassert the role of these informal mediating structures. They argued that the government's role in dealing with poverty should not be abandoned, but that it should be subordinated to the older agencies.[5]

Meanwhile, the strategies on unemployment that had guided liberals for so many years were coming under criticism from a number of black intellectuals. Among the critics was William Julius Wilson, the black chairman of the sociology department at the University of Chicago. Wilson, in his book *The Declining Significance of Race,* argued that the central problem faced by the black underclass was a structural change in the economy that tended to put a premium on the skilled worker and locked out those without skills. Wilson saw little value in affirmative action programs that emphasized quotas and tended to help better-trained middle-class blacks. Instead, he supported government planning and regulation to relieve the problems of the poor and disadvantaged. But several conservative black economists, including Walter Williams and Thomas Sowell, felt that big government itself was the problem. Williams argued that heavy government regulation of the economy had made it difficult, if not impossible, for poorer blacks to break into the mainstream. As one example, he pointed to the small number of black taxicab operators in New York City, where the cost of the medallion necessary to operate a cab was as much as $60,000, compared to the considerably larger number of black cab drivers in Washington, D.C., where the entry cost was substantially lower. Williams's most controversial proposal was to give small-scale employers an exemption from paying the minimum wage. The minimum wage, he argued, tended to reduce the number of jobs generated by small-scale or marginal employers who needed low costs to survive and grow.[6] More jobs, even at low wages, would help to solve the problem of high unemployment among black teenagers. "A rapidly growing economy solves many social ills," Williams declared.[7]

This emphasis on the private sector stood in sharp contrast to the policies and programs of liberal and Jewish groups. Conscious of the waste and suffering associated with capitalism's development, they had spent considerable time and effort trying to curb its harsher aspects. Without attempting to rewrite that stark history, a new group of intellectuals that included Irving Kristol, Milton Friedman, Michael Novak, and Paul Johnson argued that American capitalism had been given a bum rap.[8] They saw capitalism as responsible for the great material well-being enjoyed by most Americans, an affluence that even the poor shared in. In books, articles, seminars, and conferences, they argued that democratic capitalism (as they preferred to call it) was not merely a means of producing goods and services but a cultural system as well. Johnson located the "moral" origins of capitalism in powerful impulses toward privacy, liberty, and self-determination, while Novak expressed esteem for capitalism's non-utopian view of human nature. Reflecting the new mood, Joseph Epstein, editor of the *American Scholar,* announced only half-facetiously, "I just do not despise capitalism the way I once did. I do not say that I love it, but, no argument about it, the old hatred is no longer there." Kristol was aware, however, that a "survival of the fittest" form of capitalism did not appeal to most people. A market economy could succeed only when it conformed to moral conventions.

The Education Morass

A number of black intellectuals now began to challenge the traditional civil rights strategy of school desegregation as a way of improving the education of minorities. Derrick A. Bell, for example, a former NAACP lawyer and later dean of the Oregon Law School, called attention to the increasing number of black parents who were questioning the idea of busing their children out of their neighborhoods and sought instead the improvement of neighborhood schools.[9] Simultaneously, educational sociologist James Coleman, whose massive study of public education in the early 1960s had spurred the school desegregation movement, noted in a new analysis that the heavy focus on racial balance in the schools was contributing to "white flight" and making the situation in urban centers much worse.[10]

The liberal response to the problem consisted mainly of renewed calls for desegregation, additional government spending, and opposition to the idea (advanced from both the Left by Christopher Jencks and the Right by Milton Friedman) of giving vouchers or tax credits to families whose children were attending private or parochial schools. Arguing that children were being cheated by a public school system that was being dragged down by a massive bureaucracy and antiquated credentialing practices, California law professor John Coons sought legislation for a statewide system of vouchers. In the U.S. Senate, Daniel P. Moynihan of New York and Robert Packwood of Oregon introduced legislation to permit parents to deduct a portion of their expenses in sending their children to private and parochial schools.

These ideas, while initially unsuccessful, were attempts to meet the growing interest in alternatives to public education, particularly for poor or minority children. With the decline in the quality of public schools, increasing numbers of black and lower middle-class parents were sending their children to private or parochial schools. Some 78 per cent of the parochial school students in Manhattan during the 1976-77 school year were black, Hispanic, Oriental, or members of another minority. In sixty-four of the seventy-seven Catholic elementary schools in Manhattan and the Bronx, half of the students were in families with incomes at or below the poverty level. And black children constituted 73 per cent of the parochial school population in the District of Columbia. By the early eighties, Catholic schools had become in some communities the private schools of the poor.[11]

Moreover, these schools were getting good grades from some educators. In a study published in 1982, Coleman and his associates concluded that Catholic and other private high schools, despite larger classes, low-salaried teachers, and fewer resources, were doing a better job than the typical public high school. The Coleman group did not suggest the abandonment of public education, but did suggest that public schools should emulate certain aspects of private education—particularly greater emphasis on the basics, and a more orderly and disciplined learning environment. Coleman and his associates also supported tuition tax credits, not only as a way of giving disadvantaged students a wider choice of educational institutions but also to insure competition.[12]

Organizations of public school teachers countered, not without justification, that private schools were not required, like public schools, to take all applicants. They also noted that private schools could get rid of disruptive students more easily. Last but not least, defenders of public education expressed fear that any diversion of funds would further weaken public schools.

Reexamination of Life-styles

The life-styles and values associated with the turbulent sixties also came under closer scrutiny in the 1970s. James Q. Wilson, for example, focused on the broader social currents which he saw as having facilitated the growth of crime.[13] He noted that crime rates had remained stable or had declined during the period of the Great Depression, but had risen sharply in the prosperous sixties, notwithstanding significant civil rights advances. Wilson argued that crime had been restrained in the earlier period by a civilizing process often mocked as "bourgeois" but which nevertheless had worked. "Popular literature emphasized the values of thrift, order, industriousness, sobriety, the mastery of passions, and a deep regard for the future." Conduct might depart from these standards, Wilson said, but there was widespread recognition that such conduct *was* a departure and needed correction.

Although Wilson conceded that there were other factors in the rise of crime, including the abandonment of the inner cities by the middle class, both black and white, he saw a "self-expression ethic" as, in large measure, responsible for the rise. Wilson was not alone in criticizing the change in life-styles. Christopher Lasch called it the "culture of narcissism"; Tom Wolfe, the "me-decade"; and Michael Harrington noted the "slack, hedonistic and thoughtless atheism . . . of Western society."

Meanwhile, Betty Friedan, once considered the "mother" of the feminist movement, took issue with the most radical feminist ideas— that sexual differentiation inexorably produced sexual inequality, that having children was a form of female bondage, and that the family was society's chief means of oppressing women. A number of studies argued that illicit sex and violence on television and in films tended to trivialize attitudes about rape and create callous attitudes about sex.[14]

The Jewish Response

What was occurring was a major re-examination of public policy that called into question many of the views of American liberalism and its staunchest supporter, the Jewish community. The tendency among many Jews was to dismiss this as a "conservative" backlash, even though criticism was coming from all sides of the social and political spectrum, and from a number of the architects of earlier social changes. The successes of Jewish groups on matters of public policy in the postwar era stemmed from identification with the American sense of fair play and justice. Equally important, however, was their anticipation of changes in the social and political consensus. How, then, did the Jewish community respond to the new critique of liberalism? Reactions varied, but on the whole Jewish attitudes changed very little in the late seventies and early eighties.

The Welfare State

As large cities plunged deeper into fiscal crisis and the Social Security and Medicare trust funds moved toward insolvency, most Jewish groups continued to call for higher federal spending. The American Jewish Committee (AJC) and the Union of American Hebrew Congregations (UAHC) were outspoken in their criticism of the federal government's handling of New York's financial problems in 1975. The AJC and the NAACP joined in appealing to President Ford to reconsider his position on federal assistance to the city.[15] Indeed, some Jewish groups called for increased government spending programs. The United Synagogue suggested a "restructuring of social and economic programs designed to achieve full employment and, if ultimately necessary, a program of public works undertaken by government agencies as employers of last resort. . . ."

One matter of particular concern to Jewish organizations was health care. In 1975 the UAHC urged the creation of a "national comprehensive pre-paid single-benefit standard health insurance program with no deductible to cover prevention, treatment, and rehabilitation in all fields of health care." Similarly, the NJCRAC in 1976 backed "a comprehensive national health insurance program providing universal coverage" and continued to press for it in subsequent years. A new element here was increased awareness of the financial problems of the Jewish poor and elderly. In 1978 the NJCRAC commended the Carter administration's attention to urban affairs but regretted that this attention did not result in a "massive expansion of federal intervention."[16]

With the advent of the first Reagan administration, there was some recognition among Jews that the 1980 election constituted, to some degree, a popular revolution. "No one can deny the necessity of trimming the fat off the U.S. budget in order to induce future economic growth," a 1981 resolution of the Federation of Reconstructionist Congregations and Havurot declared. And at the end of a lengthy 1982 resolution decrying cutbacks in job training, food aid subsidies, housing assistance, and other federal programs, the Central Conference of American Rabbis (CCAR) agreed that the private sector was the country's primary vehicle for the creation of jobs and the elimination of poverty. It urged the government "to make every effort to encourage risk capital to greater investment in an ever expanding economy, to encourage American labor to greater productivity . . . and promotion of technological and economic expansion . . . [to promote] the welfare of all."

But such statements were few in number, grudging concessions to the popular mood. While the section on Social and Economic Justice in the NJCRAC's 1980-81 plan urged the study of means for "easing the burden of inflation and rising taxes on the middle class . . . ," it added that the purpose of such relief would be to reduce middle-class "hostility toward government programs for the disadvantaged." One would think that easing the tax burden on the middle class might have been considered a worthy end in itself. Instead, the middle class seemed to be seen as an entity whose defining quality was its "hostility" to government-sponsored efforts to aid the disadvantaged.

Having made a bow toward the resentments felt by many Americans, the NJCRAC served up a rehash of the liberal agenda. The organization's 1980-81 plan called for a national health insurance program, increased federal aid to public education, and "accelerated desegregation of public schools," even though the number of white students in most large city schools continued to drop, making the achievement of desegregation harder than ever. The 1981-82 plan extolled the virtues of a wide range of federal welfare programs, including aid to families with dependent children, food stamps, school lunches, CETA, Medicaid, housing and community development, and legal services to the poor. Meanwhile, the CCAR noted that "the majority of people living below the poverty line are women" and was highly critical of "a national fiscal policy which will lock women into the cycle of poverty." The CCAR was seemingly oblivious to the fact that many of those in poverty were unwed mothers, and that it was not "fiscal policy" that was producing illegitimate children. Significantly, both the Urban League and the NAACP were beginning to turn their attention to the problem of poor female-headed households and teenage pregnancy, having become aware that solutions to these problems were among "the most important items on the civil rights agenda today."[17]

As the 1982 recession deepened and unemployment among the non-traditional poor increased, the CCAR argued that "our government must assume responsibility for fostering employment opportunities." Distressed at the large numbers of black and Hispanic youth "out of work, out of hope, and out of faith," Albert Vorspan called upon the Jewish community "to keep alive the quality of rachmunut [pity] and justice which sear our faith and our people."[18]

This appeal for compassion, echoed by many other Jewish organizations, was clearly in line with *tzedaka,* the traditional Jewish view that it is necessary to help the poor and the needy. But according to Maimonides, the highest of the eight degrees of *tzedaka* was in helping the poor become independent, thereby preserving their dignity. What the Jewish organizations failed to acknowledge was that many of the programs they sought to protect, however well-intentioned, provided no answer to the problems posed by a growing underclass.

The Reagan administration could legitimately be criticized for some of its cutbacks. These, the non-partisan Congressional Budget Office found in 1983, hit programs benefiting low-income families twice as hard as others. Although government aid to the poorest of the poor did not change significantly, assistance to those teetering on the edge of poverty—large families with only a single breadwinner—was reduced. Tax breaks for higher income groups and big business were more generous than for those at the bottom of the social scale. If Jewish groups were fixated on governmental solutions to social problems, the Reagan administration was at the opposite extreme, causing even conservative columnist George Will to see in the Reagan initiatives a "tone of dogmatic disparagement of government . . . that suggests that all cuts are morally easy because government cannot do anything right."[19]

But one finds in the positions taken by most of the Jewish groups an unwillingness to consider changing any aspect of the welfare state, however minor. "Against corporate immorality and the venality of the privileged," Reform's Eugene B. Borowitz declared in the 1980 *Commentary* symposium, "all we can count on are proxy fights and public outrage—or government."[20] Well into the 1980s, most Jewish organizations continued to give their allegiance to the liberal-Left tradition that favors government over private sector solutions and systematically discounts what people, through their own efforts, can do for themselves. There has been little Jewish recognition of the importance of human-scale institutions and the role they might play, in cooperation with government, in resolving social problems. This is ironic, since much of the strength of the Jewish community comes from a network of Jewish federations, community centers, old-age homes, and other communal institutions. There has even been some disposition among Jews to disparage or gloss over volunteerism and privatism. And they rarely acknowledge that cutting government expenditures reduces inflation, which is one of the best things that can be done for the poor.

Social Justice Concerns

Although Jews in the United States have gained greater acceptance and greater affluence in the forty years since the end of World War II, they have been reluctant to be seen as moving away from their earlier desire for social justice. Thus, during the late 1970s and early 1980s the CCAR, the NJCRAC, and most other Jewish groups continued to adopt statements in support of farm workers and braceros, closer relations with Hispanics, and recognition of the rights of American Indians. The one domestic issue that could not be escaped by means of a resolution was the matter of black-Jewish relations.

Antagonism between the two groups, particularly on the issue of quotas, had smoldered under the surface throughout the 1970s. But it broke out with great force following the resignation of Andrew Young as U.S. ambassador to the United Nations in the summer of 1979 after Young held an unauthorized meeting with a representative of the PLO. A wide range of black leaders held Jews responsible for Young's departure from that job. Relations worsened when leaders of Dr. King's old organization, the Southern Christian Leadership Conference (SCLC), and the Rev. Jesse Jackson went to the Middle East and were photographed embracing Arafat. These episodes coincided with reports by Louis Harris and other pollsters that anti-Semitism had risen significantly among younger and better-educated blacks. This was contrary to the widespread belief that prejudice declines as education increases.[21]

Jewish groups strove desperately to maintain the old liberal coalition while speaking out against anti-Jewish and anti-Israel manifestations among blacks. In the aftermath of the Young affair, a section on "anti-

Semitism in the black community" was added to the Joint Program Plan of the NJCRAC. Noting that black anti-Semitism had "created concern and anxiety among Jews," the plan went on to examine the causes of the deterioration of the old alliance, including the shift of the black struggle from the South to the North and "a growing sense of kinship among some blacks with people of the 'Third World.' " In an attempt, perhaps, to display evenhandedness, or to demonstrate continued Jewish sympathy for the poor, the plan placed a major share of the responsibility for tension on the shoulders of Jews themselves. It noted the "progressive distancing of the steadily more secure (economically) and accepted (socially) Jewish community from the problems of still relatively insecure and disadvantaged minorities" and urged "intensive interpretation within the Jewish community to overcome anti-black" animus among Jews.

When Jesse Jackson came forward as a presidential candidate in 1983, Jewish groups hesitated to criticize him despite his clear-cut record of anti-Semitic remarks (even after it was reported that Jackson had more than once used the term "Hymie" to refer to Jews) "lest we," in the words of Rabbi Schindler, president of the UAHC, "fan flames of a black-Jewish confrontation." There were some who saw in Jackson's candidacy something positive. In a speech prepared for delivery to a UAHC convention which received attention in the black press, Albert Vorspan, while uncomfortable with some of the things Jackson had said, nevertheless felt the black leader would "help expose the American people to the real world, broaden the agenda for debate . . . and extend participation in the political process."[22] It was only after Louis Farrakhan, a close political associate of Jackson's and the leader of a Black Muslim group, made a number of blatant anti-Semitic remarks that Jewish spokesmen strongly denounced Jackson and urged Democratic presidential candidate Walter Mondale to dissociate himself from Jackson. Among other things, Farrakhan referred to Judaism as a "gutter religion."

Much the same hesitation to confront the positions of friends and allies for fear of alienating them can be seen in the NJCRAC's language on racial quotas in its 1980-81 plan. Earlier, a number of Jewish community relations agencies had filed briefs before the Supreme Court opposing racial quotas in the Bakke case, but when their stand evoked a sharp response from black leaders and liberal groups, they backed off (except for the ADL). The NJCRAC was thus able to report "no consensus . . . in the Jewish community" in two cases subsequent to Bakke in which racial quotas were unquestionably at issue. In reality, there has been very strong opposition to quotas among rank-and-file Jews. In 1983 the American Jewish Committee filed a friend-of-the-court brief supporting affirmative action but opposing a proposed quota system for the promotion of black police officers in New Orleans.

Among many Jewish groups there is a widespread belief that the Reagan administration is unsympathetic to civil rights. In the summer of 1982 the CCAR criticized cuts in the budgets and staffs of federal civil rights enforcement agencies, attempts to weaken existing civil rights legislation, and the abandonment of regulations that implement nondiscriminatory legal requirements, such as prohibition of tax-exempt status for segregated educational institutions. While the administration has been insensitive on a number of civil rights issues, it has made no general attempt to reverse the civil rights gains of the past. It has sought mainly to curb what many see as excesses, such as the use of racial quotas in hiring and the busing of children to integrate schools. These are actions that most Jews support.

The civil rights issue came to a head in 1983 when President Reagan fired three members of the U.S. Commission on Civil Rights and named three replacements with strong civil rights but anti-quota records, including the former head of the American Jewish Committee, Morris B. Abram. Jewish reactions were quite divergent. The ADL, for example, supported all three of the President's nominees; the UAHC, on the other hand, was in total opposition. "It is not the independence and integrity of the nominees which is at issue," declared Vorspan, the UAHC vice president. "Rather, it is the independence and integrity of the commission that is at stake."[23] In a compromise resolution of the issue, a newly constituted commission that included several of the President's appointees promptly moved closer to a position held by the main body of Jewish public opinion by renouncing the use of quotas in a case involving the Detroit police department and urging the Supreme Court to adopt a similar position.[24]

In the summer of 1983, Jewish groups were asked by black and liberal leaders to join in a second March on Washington to commemorate the twentieth anniversary of the 1963 high point of the civil rights movement. The list of sponsors and participants included the Arab Anti-Defamation League, Jesse Jackson, the head of the SCLC, peace activists, feminists, gays, and Palestinian representatives, as well as labor, religious, and other groups associated with the earlier event. Also among them was the UAHC and its head, Rabbi Schindler. Noting this strange assortment of groups and causes, the *New Republic* commented acidly that ". . . it is another case of manipulation and exploitation of blacks with their organizational needs by whites with their organizational agendas."[25] The Urban League refused to participate, and black columnist Tony Brown called the March "a step backward from the one I attended in 1963."[26]

Jewish groups were concerned by the opposition of the sponsors of the 1983 March to the "militarization of internal conflicts, often abetted and encouraged by massive U.S. arms exports . . . [to the] Middle East and Central America, while basic human rights problems are neglected." This statement was believed to have an anti-Israel intent. The NJCRAC cautioned its members about involvement in the March and decided that non-participation did not require formal notice. A formal letter of non-participation "might be misinterpreted and perceived as confrontational, possibly leading to an exacerbation of black-Jewish tensions and causing problems at the community level," an NJCRAC official wrote to member agencies.[27]

The UAHC was eventually successful in gaining assurances that anti-Israel sentiments would be deleted from the final version of the March announcement, and that the March would emphasize the goals of peace rather than any particular strategy for achieving it. With the exception of the UAHC and the New Jewish Agenda, few Jewish organizations were involved. Unlike 1963, none of the more than sixty speakers at the March was Jewish; Rabbi Schindler was relegated to delivering the benediction. Tony Brown summarized his distaste for the March this way: "We do not speak as admirers of this administration's attitude toward civil rights. But we do think that so far as the fulfillment of Martin Luther King Jr.'s dream is concerned, anyone who believes that the Reagan government is the problem and its replacement the solution is living a different kind of dream: a pipe dream." The solution, Brown wrote, "is the economic development of the nation's 30-million-member African-American community, based on self-help."[28]

There is much to be said for efforts to preserve black-Jewish harmony. The plight of large numbers of our citizens who have suffered so cruelly down through the years must continue to touch the Jewish heart. The empathy this calls forth is fully in line with Jewish tradition, which calls for helping the disadvantaged. However, such help must be guided by a clearer recognition of the dangers posed by the anti-Jewish and anti-Israel tendencies of a segment of the black intelligentsia and the need to go beyond welfare state solutions that have been palliatives but not solutions to the underlying problems involved. This is yet to be fully understood.

The New Right

Most Jewish groups now seemed to feel that the greatest danger to civil rights and civil liberties came from the growth of the Christian Right. This growth touched a particularly sensitive nerve, since Jews have tended to measure their sense of security by the relative openness of the society in which they live. Even the more conservative Jewish groups, such as the Jewish War Veterans and the UOJC, were alarmed.[29] At its 1982 convention the UOJC expressed alarm at congressional attempts to limit the power of the federal judiciary and pledged to oppose any such efforts. "The so-called 'New Right' of today . . . has broken ranks with the responsible suggestions that authentic political conservatives have made in the past for gradual change," Rabbi Mark A. Golub wrote in a statement for the CCAR Justice and Peace Committee. At its 1981 convention the UAHC called upon public schools and library boards to resist pressures to ban certain books; the CCAR adopted a similar statement the following year.

The 1980-81 NJCRAC Joint Program Plan expressed concern about anti-Jewish sentiments expressed by Protestant evangelical clergymen, such as the widely publicized statement by the Rev. Bailey Smith, president of the Southern Baptist Convention, that "God Almighty does not hear the prayer of a Jew." Rabbi Schindler told the UAHC in 1980 "that the Jerry Falwells are deliberately fomenting anti-Jewish sentiments and violence. . . ."[30] Jews have been warned in recent years by most of their leaders not to be deceived by the support given to Israel by the Moral Majority and other Christian Right groups.

The growth and activities of the New Right, particularly the effort to "Christianize" America, do indeed pose serious and disturbing questions, both for Jews and for other Americans. However, the Jewish discussion of these questions has been defined in the narrowest terms. Anti-Semitism in the New Right has been quite minor. Since his foolish 1980 statement, Smith has made strenuous efforts to convince Jews that he did not mean it as they understood it. He subsequently visited Israel, and afterwards an ADL official attributed his remark to his narrow experience rather than to any malice toward Jews. Most recently, Falwell came before the Rabbinical Assembly and apologized for calling for the Christianizing of America.[31]

The historian Jonathan D. Sarna has argued that "Judaism—quite distinct from the liberalism of many Jews—does not require support for abortion, gay rights, or ERA. The notion that secularism and licentiousness lie at the root of the nation's ills may be right or wrong, but in no sense can it be termed anti-Jewish."[32] Jewish groups, for the most part, have failed to understand that the concerns of the New Right—apart from the unfortunate tactics sometimes employed to achieve their goals and occasional instances of anti-Semitism—are congruent with the feelings and thoughts of many Americans. There is deep concern about what Daniel J. Elazar has called "the new paganism," which has been the dominant cultural ethos in this country for a generation or more. "What gives the Moral Majority and other religious groups their clout," Burton Yale Pines wrote in 1981, "is that on many key issues the morality they proclaim is the morality of the majority."[33] By failing to recognize and deal with these concerns, Jewish groups contributed to the vacuum ultimately filled by the Moral Majority and other right-wing groups.

Abortion

Most Jewish groups agreed with the 1973 Supreme Court decision (reaffirmed in 1983) making abortion legal, and they have opposed efforts to curtail the impact of that decision. The 1981-82 plan of the NJCRAC urged Jewish organizations to "make known publicly and to members of Congress . . . their opposition to unreasonable restraints on the freedom of pregnant women to make choices as to abortion." Reform Judaism took a similar position. Women who do not adhere to any religious tradition, Rabbi Dennis Math wrote, "have a right to make up their minds on the issue based on their own personal morality,"[34] while Rabbi Schindler, in testimony before a Senate subcommittee, argued that a proposed "Human Life" bill would impinge upon Jewish practice, thereby denying Jews the opportunity to apply their faith's moral standards.

The response of Conservative Jewish bodies has been somewhat more complex. While noting that "abortions involve very serious psychological, religious, and moral problems," the United Synagogue declared in 1975 that "the welfare of the mother must always be our primary concern."[35] It therefore urged its congregations to oppose efforts to weaken the Court's decision on abortion. In a 1976 resolution, the Women's League for Conservative Judaism argued that "freedom of choice is inherent in the civil rights of women."[36] Five years later, in 1981, together with the United Synagogue and other Jewish and non-Jewish groups, the Women's League filed an *amicus curiae* brief in opposition to an Akron ordinance to restrict abortion.

But the Rabbinical Assembly remained silent until 1983, when its Committee on Jewish Law and Standards overwhelmingly adopted a statement sanctioning "abortion under some circumstances"—that is, when there was a prospect of severe physical or psychological harm to the mother, or the fetus was severely defective. The statement noted, however, that "Jewish tradition . . . does not permit abortion on demand."

The only clear opposition among Jews to the legalization of abortion has come from Orthodox groups like the UOJC and Agudath Israel. The latter termed the 1973 Court decision "an act that Torah law regards as akin to murder,"[37] while the UOJC repeated its view that "all life—including fetal life—is inviolate." It held that aborting a pregnancy "is not a private matter between a woman and her physician unless the life of the mother is involved."[38]

The great majority of Jewish groups have joined liberals and civil libertarians in decrying any return to the time when illegal backroom abortions often threatened women's lives. They are deeply concerned about bringing unwanted children into the world and the neglect that many such children would suffer. Part of the distaste felt by many Jews toward critics of abortion has been the statements of some pro-life advocates who have likened abortion to the Holocaust, who sought the imprisonment of doctors, who raided abortion clinics, or who opposed government funding of abortions for the poor.

The enthusiasm with which the movement to make abortion more readily available has been greeted by most Jewish groups and the argument that it should be available under virtually any and all circumstances ("freedom of choice") raise, however, a number of questions that are not often faced. Even if one holds that the decision to have an abortion ultimately belongs to the woman involved, in consultation with her doctor, are there not reasons to avoid having to make such a decision whenever possible? Should an abortion be undertaken by a couple in order, let us say, to purchase a second car or take a trip to Europe—in short, as a matter of convenience or even as a form of birth control? Jewish groups seem to be approaching the issue from the viewpoint of Planned Parenthood or the American Civil Liberties Union (ACLU). But Jewish groups are not Planned Parenthood or the ACLU. They were brought into existence to guard Jewish interests and bring Jewish values to bear on public policy issues.

In his book *Love and Sex,* Robert Gordis, emeritus professor of the philosophy of religion at the Jewish Theological Seminary, noted that Jewish law recognizes that the fetus is not a viable human being while in its mother's womb, since life cannot be sustained outside its natural environment there. But, he continues, the alleged right of abortion on demand, based on a view that a woman has rights over her body, "is a contention which Judaism, and indeed all high religion, must reject on both theological and ethical grounds as being essentially a pagan doctrine." Abortion should be "legally available but ethically restricted, to be practiced only for very good reasons," Gordis concludes. Echoing Gordis from a secular viewpoint, the *New Republic* said that "we agree with the Court that a woman has a legal right to an abortion, though we would hope it is a right that will never be exercised."[39]

Beyond the broader moral or ethical question, there is another issue involved. According to the Center for Disease Control, there were 1.3 million abortions in 1980, slightly more than one abortion for every three live births.[40] One might well ask what kind of society can lightly accept such irreverence for life. A society that has witnessed the dramatic growth of abortion, a sharp rise in violence and crime, the appearance of pornography as legitimate business, and other evidences of the new paganism governing American life today bears a striking resemblance to Weimar Germany in the 1920s that might well give Jews concern.

Increasingly, blacks have been asking far more fundamental questions on the abortion issue. At an important and highly publicized "Black Family Summit Meeting" in the spring of 1984, the emphasis was not on making abortion easier but on how to change attitudes in the community with regard to family responsibility through a self-help strategy. "We may have allowed our just anger at what America has done to obscure our own need for self-discipline and community values," said John Jacob, head of the Urban League, in his address at the meeting. "In concentrating on the wrongs of discrimination and poverty, we may have neglected the fact that there is a lot we can do about our own problems ourselves." He called for the "relevance and imagination of our organizations" in the face of the family crisis in changing attitudes in communities where prevailing expectations and individual achievements are built up or else eroded.

Asked why Jewish organizations have not dealt with questions of greater sexual discipline, Rabbi Balfour Brickner responded, "Right now I have to fight the '3-H Team,'" a reference to Senators Helms and Hatch and Congressman Hyde. "Once that threat is overcome, I can deal with these issues," Brickner said.[41] Such questions, however, are central to the issue of abortion. They are deeply troubling to many Americans and, as has been suggested, provide a fertile ground for the inroads made by the Radical Right in American life.

Prayer and Bible-Reading

Jewish organizations have been deeply disturbed by the efforts of the Christian Right to return prayer and Bible-reading to the schools. They see this as a violation of the principle of separation of church and state. President Reagan added to their concern by endorsing a constitutional amendment to permit organized prayer. A bill that would have started the amending process was defeated in the Senate early in 1984. The Synagogue Council and the NJCRAC along with the Baptist Joint Committee on Public Affairs, the National Coalition for Public Education and Religious Liberty, and the National Council of Churches opposed the amendment. The NJCRAC explained its stand this way:

> Religious observances in the public schools of our religiously pluralistic communities are unwarranted and imprudent. They violate the rights of those children and those parents whose religious or philosophical convictions may be offended by the particular observance or by any religious observance. They may cause emotional distress in those children who must choose between participating despite conscientious scruples and making themselves conspicuous by not participating.[42]

The removal of religious symbols from public schools and other public areas continues to be a matter "demanding sustained attention," according to the NJCRAC. An entire section of its 1980-81 plan was devoted to opposing such manifestations of religion in public schools as the posting of the Ten Commandments and the singing of Christmas carols.

Jewish fears were brought to a high point during the 1984 election campaign, which saw the heavy intrusion of religious issues. They were especially troubled by President Reagan's address before a prayer breakfast in Dallas in which he charged that those who opposed such expressions of religion as voluntary prayer in public schools were "intolerant of religion." Rabbi Mordecai Waxman, the president of the Synagogue Council, among others, was highly critical, arguing that religion is and should be a private commitment.[43]

Jewish organizations fear that efforts to restore Bible-reading and prayer may "Christianize" the public schools, that even small transgressions of the separation principle may lead to larger ones. But in the debate between sectarianism and secularism, Jews have tended to side with secularism. They have failed to see the "tolerant, non-coercive, and inclusive" civil religion which, Charles Krauthammer argues, has infused American life with "a sense of transcendence."[44] This civil religion was the driving force, for example, behind Dr. King's extraordinary "I Have a Dream" speech. But Jews have been so concerned about violations of the church-state separation principle that they have objected to any common-core aspects of the Western religious tradition that may show up in public education; they are unwilling to countenance even "a moment of silence" in schools. (In discussing this issue, columnist George Will asked, ". . . since when is it any 'injury' to be offended by what might be going on in someone's head?"[45]) It may be that the singing of "Adeste Fideles" or the posting of the Ten Commandments on the walls of public schools are not the crucial problems that some Jewish groups make them out to be. What may constitute a far more serious threat to Jews, but one which goes largely unnoticed by them, is the breakdown in societal norms.

To be sure, displaying the Ten Commandments would not, in itself, be a major blow against the "new paganism." Nevertheless, the elimination of religious symbols of decency may have contributed to the decline in morality. "It is a mistake to assume that rejecting the lunacy of the far Right means we must deny the value to society of a religious sensibility," Krauthammer has written. The connection between social pathology and the decline of the "religious sensibility" has been commented upon by such diverse figures as Arthur Schlesinger, Jr., and Aleksandr Solzhenitsyn. It may be that in the mid-1980s it has become urgent to find new ways to encourage the forces that contribute to order and stability. The inability of most Jewish groups to realize this is a major failure.

Human Rights Abroad

Jewish organizations have been active in defending civil liberties and minority rights in foreign countries for much the same reasons that they have done so in the United States—a perceived self-interest combined with a moral concern for the oppressed that grows out of the Jewish experience. Thus, attention has been focused on the persecution of Jews in Iran, the Arab countries, Argentina, and the Soviet Union, where Jews seeking to emigrate lose their jobs or suffer other forms of harassment.

But the record is also filled with statements on broader concerns. American Jews have consistently supported Third World countries in their efforts to achieve control of their economic and political destinies, and they have continually called for the protection of personal dignity, including, in the words of a 1978 Synagogue Council statement, "freedom from torture, cruel or degrading treatment, and arbitrary arrest or imprisonment." A number of Jewish groups commended President Carter for drawing public attention to human rights violations abroad during his administration.

Nor have Jewish organizations been indifferent, as sometimes charged, to violations of human rights by left-wing regimes. The CCAR, for example, was highly critical of the Cambodian government in 1976 for the brutal death of millions of its subjects, as was the UOJC two years later. Jewish religious organizations have been active in relief and resettlement programs for refugees from Indochina. In 1980 the CCAR called for a boycott of the Olympic games in Moscow not only because of the Soviet Union's "contempt for . . . human, social, and religious rights" internally but also because of Soviet expansionist policies. Two years later the organization expressed concern about "recent acts of Soviet oppression," singling out the violence practiced against the people of Afghanistan and the repression of the human and civil rights of the Polish people.

At the same time, however, it is clear that many Jewish organizations have paid more attention to human rights violations by right-wing regimes associated with the United States. Rabbi David Saperstein, codirector of the Reform movement's Religious Action Center, declares that this state of affairs comes about because "our government tends to support dictatorships of the right more than it supports dictatorships of the left."[46] Perhaps the most consistent targets of the Jewish organizations have been the apartheid policies of South Africa and that country's relationship with the United States. Over the years the NJCRAC has argued that South Africa is a "totalitarian" country and has urged the U.S. government to support U.N. sanctions against it. Similar arguments have been made by the CCAR and other Jewish groups.[47] More recently, much effort has been aimed at halting U.S. investments in, and trade with, South Africa. Typical was a 1979 statement by the UAHC that urged American business firms in South Africa to leave that country unless the government changes its racial policies.

Jewish religious bodies have also condemned human rights violations in Central America by regimes supported by the United States.[48] The UAHC has been especially critical in demanding the termination of all military assistance to El Salvador and the withdrawal from that country of all foreign military personnel and advisors.[49] For all practical purposes, this would simply insure a unilateral U.S. withdrawal, since Soviet and Cuban military support in the area is not subject to such calls. Views like these have brought Jewish and other religious groups into sharp collision with the Reagan administration.

This was graphically illustrated in 1983 at a meeting of Jewish leaders with Elliott Abrams, assistant secretary of state for human rights and humanitarian affairs, and one of the contributors to the 1980

Commentary symposium on liberalism and the Jews. Abrams said he wanted "to avoid utopianism and to deal with the world as it exists." He argued that the Reagan administration's commitment to human rights had been expressed through quiet diplomatic pressure to release political prisoners, which had effected some improvement. Pointing to the support the Sandinista government in Nicaragua was receiving from the Soviet Union, Abrams rejected the view "now fashionable in some liberal circles" that the Sandinistas "represented progress and reform."

In response, Rabbi Arthur Hertzberg said he was "frightened to the very marrow of my bones" by the Reagan administration's approach to human rights. Hertzberg claimed that the United States was sending foreign governments this message: "If you are for us, all your sins will be forgiven. If you are not, we will point out every one of your human rights violations and beat up on you." A representative of Emunah Women of America called the administration's policies "almost hypocritical." Someone from the American Jewish Committee asked, "Where is our pressure to change the situation in South Africa?"[50]

As has been pointed out, human rights violations touch an unusually sensitive nerve in the Jewish community. In the positions of some Jewish religious groups, however, one senses a high moral stance taken with little regard for reality in complex situations where civil war also involves Communist efforts to make further headway in the Western hemisphere. These efforts went so far in Grenada that one independent investigator who examined captured documents following the American invasion declared that "Cuba was running Grenada."[51]

The Nicaraguan government is led by indigenous Marxist-Leninists supported by thousands of Cuban trainers, teachers, and supervisors, including 2,000 military advisors. Moreover, Nicaragua is receiving considerable assistance from the Soviet Union, Libya, and the PLO.[52] El Salvador is not a model democracy, but its government has been selected through popular election. Former U.N. ambassador Jeane J. Kirkpatrick contends that El Salvador's guerrillas are directed from Nicaragua, are armed with Soviet weapons, and are bent on establishing a one-party dictatorship similar to the one in Nicaragua.[53] ("We guide ourselves by the scientific doctrines of the Revolution, by Marxist-Leninism," Nicaraguan minister of defense Humberto Ortega told his army. ". . . Our political force is Sandinismo and our doctrine is

Marxist Leninism."[54]) Even the left-wing Honduran writer Rodolfo Pastor has noted that Nicaragua's armed-camp mentality creates an atmosphere "in which the highest civic virtue is submission to discipline and the worst sin is open political disagreement." The Administration's policies in Central America have not ignored the underlying social and economic causes of discontent. While it is clear that the United States has provided substantial military support to the countries of Central America, two out of every three U.S. dollars going into the region by the spring of 1983 were in the form of economic aid.

Were it heeded, the effect of the attack by many Jewish and other groups on American policy in Central America would be a unilateral abrogation of U.S. responsibility to its allies under the OAS Charter. Such action would jeopardize this country's interests and probably be counter to popular feeling both in the United States and in Central America. Through their criticism, Jewish and other groups have sought to give vent to their emotions rather than come to grips with the difficulties of a complex situation. This may be understandable in the light of Jewish experience, but it oversimplifies the issues involved. What George Will said of Americans more generally can also be said of American Jews: "They have never liked the language of power in diplomacy, preferring the language of ideals, such as human rights."[55]

National Defense

Over the years, Jews in the United States have taken strong positions on war and disarmament. With the defeat of the Axis powers in 1945, Albert Einstein recalled the earlier dream of a world without war, united under a world government that would outlaw the use of weapons of mass destruction. "We scientists," he wrote, "whose tragic destiny it has been to help make the methods of annihilation ever more gruesome and more effective, must consider it our solemn and transcendent duty to do all in our power in preventing these weapons from being used for the brutal purpose for which they were intended."[56]

In *Jewish Values and Social Crisis* (1968), Albert Vorspan traced classical Jewish views on war. He attempted to strike a balance, but the anti-war theme is dominant. (Among the quotations from Jewish tradition, twenty are clearly unsympathetic to war, while only five—e.g., "the Lord is a man of war" [Exodus 15:3]—can be said to present war in a favorable light.)⁵⁷ Resolutions adopted by Jewish religious groups throughout the 1960s and 1970s—the civic agencies were somewhat more reluctant to speak out—called for waging peace to eliminate the threat of war and hailed efforts by the Soviet Union and the United States to negotiate weapons reductions. In 1971 the United Synagogue urged the establishment of a Department of Peace devoted to "research, planning, training, and education for the peaceful resolution of international conflicts."

An important element in Jewish thought has been that money not used for defense could be utilized for social problems. Our government should "reduce our defense expenditures" and "reorder our national priorities" in order to deal "effectively with the crisis of our cities and with the worldwide problems of poverty," the Synagogue Council declared in 1969. In 1975 the CCAR sought a cut in defense spending, but without, of course, "withdrawing support for democratic nations including Israel."⁵⁸

In actions like these, Jewish groups were following broader anti-war currents that had been flowing in the United States since 1945. One example was the quick demobilization of the U.S. military after World War II that had the effect of encouraging Soviet expansion. Later, the Viet Nam war brought home to many Americans both the horrors of war and a desire to avoid all but the most necessary foreign commitments. It is, therefore, not surprising that the U.S. military position gradually deteriorated or that Jimmy Carter pledged to cut defense spending when he ran for president in 1976. In October 1982 the *New York Times* reported that during the preceding thirty years the numbers of U.S. warplanes, ships, tanks, guns, and other non-nuclear weapons had all declined from their 1952 levels. Along with reductions in the numbers of weapons came a decline in operational readiness. The clear implication of the article was that the countries of Western Europe had gradually become more dependent on U.S. nuclear weapons to deter Soviet aggression, and the United States and its NATO allies would probably be overwhelmed in a conventional war.

Although the United States abandoned large quantities of chemical weapons and ceased developing new types of intercontinental ballistic missiles (ICBMs) during the 1970s, the Soviet Union did just the opposite. The Soviets continued to develop, produce, and deploy chemical weapons, and they also developed four new generations of

ICBMs. This gave them a significant advantage over the United States in total "throw weight," and a great and threatening superiority in Europe.[59] Meanwhile, the Soviets also began deploying a large number of intermediate-range SS-20 nuclear missiles that could be used against the Europeans.[60] This deployment could hardly be seen simply as a defensive reaction against potential enemies, given that during the 1970s the Western allies had, in comparative terms, been disarming.

"Since 1945 there has been a relentless expansion of the Soviet sphere of influence," Andrei Sakharov has written. ". . . Objectively, this is nothing but Soviet expansion on a world scale. This process has spread as the U.S.S.R. has grown stronger economically . . . and in scientific, technological, and military terms. . . ."[61]

Except for an isolated resolution or two critical of Soviet behavior, however, Jewish religious leaders either seemed to be unaware of the problem or focused their concerns elsewhere. When the Carter and the Reagan administrations made crash efforts to increase U.S. military strength following the Soviet invasion of Afghanistan, Reform leadership was especially critical. Vorspan told a High Holy Day Leadership Conference in 1982 that "social decency has been traded for 1.5 trillion dollars for the next five years in arms budgets. That's a tinder box and not safe for Jews."[62] In 1982 a Reconstructionist synagogue on Long Island decried the "guns over butter" approach in a resolution addressed to its national organization: ". . . bombs and missiles must not be allowed to replace school lunches and the capability to buy homes." Indeed, Reform Judaism seemed to think that the deterioration in relations with the Soviet Union was caused largely by U.S. policy. After stating that military spending adds no new goods to the economy and is inflationary, the UAHC declared in 1981 that military registration and a draft were "both unnecessary and unnecessarily provocative, reflective of a national trend toward increased militarism that threatens world peace."[63] The New Jewish Agenda, operating from a leftist perspective, declared in 1982 that increases in the defense budget were an "effort to maximize profits," and the following year a group of Jewish artists and entertainers joined conductor Leonard Bernstein in his birthday pleas for worldwide disarmament.[64]

One of the ironies in the position taken by Jewish religious organizations on matters of defense and rearmament is that it overlooks the close connection between American military power and the security of

Israel. Indeed, during the Yom Kippur War the Israeli army fired shells that had been unloaded from U.S. planes only hours earlier. If there had been no American shells and no Flying Boxcars, Israel might have perished. "To survive," Milton Himmelfarb has said, "Israel needs the American arsenal full."[65]

The recognition that U.S. military might is closely related to its ability to support Israel has made Jewish civic organizations reluctant to enter the debate over defense expenditures. In January 1981, as the Reagan administration took office, the NJCRAC issued a statement that recommended the "establishment of U.S. military facilities" in the Middle East and urged Jewish agencies to support "defense programs to achieve this goal." The statement, however, avoided endorsing any specific amount of money to underwrite the recommendation. To appease the "butter" side of the debate, the summary of the session reported that there was also fear that "an increased defense budget can adversely affect our relationship with other constituencies with whom we work on domestic issues."

Nuclear Freeze Proposal

It seems clear that if the United States and the Soviet Union engaged in a general nuclear war, there would be no winner—only unimaginable destruction and chaos. The anxiety engendered by awareness that such a war could take place resulted in both spontaneous and carefully orchestrated efforts in the United States and in Western Europe to impose a "freeze" on further building, testing, and deployment of nuclear weapons, particularly when the United States, in agreement with its NATO allies, prepared to place Pershing II and cruise missiles on European soil to counter the overwhelming superiority of Soviet SS-20 missiles.

The nuclear freeze movement in the United States was welcomed by the Soviet Union, and a series of articles in the *New York Times* in 1983 described the efforts of the Soviet intelligence arm, the KGB, to capitalize on it in Europe. Vladimir Bukovsky documented the Soviet role in organizing the movement in the May 1982 issue of *Commentary*. While the freeze movement has influenced but not determined American defense policy, no comparable movement exists—or could exist—within the U.S.S.R. that could moderate Soviet policies. Critics like Solzhenitsyn and Sakharov have been exiled or silenced. In an article smuggled out of the Soviet Union and published in *Foreign Affairs* in the summer of 1983, Sakharov argued that the United States might have to match the Soviet Union in nuclear weapons before arms negotiations to ease tensions between the two countries could achieve any concrete results. As long as the Soviet Union leads in land-based missiles, Sakharov wrote, "there is very little chance of its relinquishing that lead." The article appeared at about the same time that the Harvard Nuclear Study Group published *Living With Nuclear Weapons*. In that book, Derek Bok, president of Harvard, and a group of international-affairs experts argued that a policy of nuclear deterrence, though unappealing, is for the moment inescapable.

Jewish religious and civic organizations were relatively slow to join the nuclear freeze movement. But when the Catholic bishops took the lead in support of the freeze, Jewish groups quickly joined the debate. At its annual convention in 1982, the CCAR found itself "inspired by the prophets" to note that even a limited nuclear war "would result in death, injury, and disease on a scale without precedent." It called upon the U.S. and Soviet governments to adopt a mutual freeze on the testing, production, and deployment of nuclear weapons and new delivery systems. The following year it renewed its call, adding an appeal that the United States pledge not to be the first country to use nuclear weapons. The UAHC announced a nationwide campaign in the spring of 1983 to mobilize support for ending the nuclear arms race and published a thick compendium of articles called *Preventing the Nuclear Holocaust: A Jewish Response*. In April of that year the Rabbinical Assembly called for "a bilateral, mutually verifiable total cessation of the production and deployment of nuclear weapons." The UOJC made a similar plea.[66]

Earlier in 1983, the Synagogue Council of America (SCA) placed the Jewish religious community's seal of approval on the nuclear freeze movement. The SCA avoided using the word "freeze," however, apparently because it did not want to endorse any particular approach, especially a unilateral U.S. freeze.[67] A wide array of other Jewish groups also joined the freeze movement, including the newly formed and left-wing New Jewish Agenda, the Council of Jewish Federations, and B'nai B'rith, one of the largest mass membership organizations. Agudath Israel, however, held back, declaring it an oversimplification of Jewish tradition to interpret reverence for life as an argument for a nuclear freeze. "Peace is a religious imperative," Agudath Israel declared, but "so is a strong national defense."[68]

Believing that a new approach was needed to end the impasse on nuclear weapons between the U.S.S.R. and the United States, the Reconstructionist movement created the Shalom Center to study nuclear policy issues and appointed Arthur Waskow, an early leader in the left-wing Institute for Policy Studies, to head it.[69] Waskow and the New Jewish Agenda traced their roots back to the civil rights and anti-Viet Nam war movements. The latter's approach to defense and nuclear weapons issues was based on the view that the arms race was at least partly the result of "narrow concepts of masculinity and femininity, limiting our ability to be fully human . . . and irrational fear of same-sex relationships." "The glorification of so-called 'masculine' virtues of competition and aggression has contributed to the militarism which has brought the human race to the brink of self-destruction," the New Jewish Agenda concluded in 1982.

It is significant that most of the Western European states have accepted as necessary the deployment of American medium-range missiles on their soil.[70] Nevertheless, the idea of nuclear parity in Western Europe seems unconvincing to many Americans, who contend that since one Trident submarine could cause so much destruction in the Soviet Union, that country would not take advantage of its superiority in intermediate missiles. But this argument misses the point. Since nuclear warfare is "unthinkable," and since the Soviet Union has far superior conventional military forces, the U.S.S.R. could bring Western Europe to its knees simply by threatening an invasion. Solzhenitsyn has explained how:

> At one time there was no comparison between the strength of the USSR and yours. Then it became equal. . . . Perhaps today it is just greater than balance, but soon it will be two to one. Then three to one. Finally it will be five to one. . . . With such a nuclear superiority it will be possible to block the use of your weapons, and on some unlucky morning they will declare: "Attention. We're marching our troops to Europe, and if you make a move, we will annihilate you." And this ratio of three to one, of five to one, will have its effect: you will not make a move.[71]

None of the Jewish groups has called for additional funds to build up U.S. conventional forces to counter this threat. Indeed, the opposite has been true. It has been left to the non-establishment Agudath Israel to warn that while "no stone should be left unturned in an effort to put a halt to the frightening arms race and to achieve genuine peace," this can only be achieved through strength. Contending that arguments for a freeze have been a "misuse of Jewish tradition," the organization has asked, "Who is to say whether more nuclear arms or disarmament is the ultimate vehicle to peace?"[72]

CHAPTER FIVE

The Utopian Dilemma

Until the recent past our obligations to the Jewish people and to all humanity seemed congruent. At times now these two perspectives appear to conflict. We must, however, confront them without abandoning either of our commitments. Judaism calls us simultaneously to universal and particular obligations.
REFORM JUDAISM: A CENTENARY PERSPECTIVE, 1976[1]

WHAT CAN BE SAID ABOUT the nature and direction of American Judaism with respect to public policy today? In the main, Jewish religious and civic organizations have struggled to respond to the public issues of the last thirty years in ways consistent with Judaism's humane and liberal tradition. For the most part, one does not find in American Judaism a sharp cleavage like that between the National Council of Churches and the majority of Protestant Christians, or between the Catholic hierarchy and Catholic laity, although the formation in recent years of both the Jewish Institute for National Security Affairs (JINSA) and the New Jewish Agenda indicates that mainstream Jewish bodies are not without Jewish critics. Nor has American Judaism experienced the degree of radicalization found in Protestant bodies or among the advocates of "liberation theology" in the Roman Catholic Church.

Jewish organizations have sought to ground their positions in the prophetic tradition and traditional Jewish law. Their statements often acknowledge religious authority or precedent before going on to make essentially political pronouncements. "They seem more often related to editorials in the *Washington Post* and *New York Times* than to halakah," says Rabbi Joshua Haberman, senior rabbi at the Washington Hebrew Congregation.[2] The resolutions and statements of the major Jewish organizations are subject to the same kind of criticism that Ernest W. Lefever has directed at the World Council of Churches,[3] and that Father Avery Dulles[4] and J. Brian Benestad[5] have made of the pronouncements of the U.S. Catholic bishops: the authors of the statements lack sufficient expertise to speak with authority about many of the highly technical questions which they address, and they introduce "their own political and economic biases, which should on no account be confused with the teaching of the church." Lucy Dawidowicz has suggested that "Jewish life in the last few decades has been monopolized by rabbis with such single-minded dedication to nationalism and social justice that we have become unaccustomed to rabbis who place God above His people."[6]

The Jewish Tradition

In all fairness, it should be pointed out that few contemporary issues can be resolved by immediate reference to traditional Jewish sources. "Judaism certainly has something to say about every significant issue in life," Rabbi Norman Lamm wrote almost a generation ago, "but this judgment can be meaningful only if it is applied to a problem that has been properly defined." Thus, the Jewish tradition defines war as bad and peace as good; it argues that fairness and justice should prevail among nations. But whether placing Pershing II missiles in Western Europe helps or hinders peace cannot be determined from religious teachings. With respect to an issue like this, one is arguing not principle or theology, but political realities and prudence. Seymour Siegel warned in 1961 that "social action . . . had been relegated to the periphery" of Jewish life and called for greater involvement in societal problems. He added, however, that "concern for the solution of social issues is not enough. It must be coupled with intelligence." ". . . Teachers of morality must not only be fired by idealism; they must also be instructed by realism."[7] And Rabbi Lamm warned that "naïveté in proposing simplistic solutions to enormously complex international issues and the almost incredible chutzpah in labeling one's prejudices as official 'Judaism' point to the danger of making religion too relevant."[8]

This is not to deny that religion should have some influence over secular affairs. Such intervention, however, calls for great care in dealing with the moral issues involved. Whether or not the nation seeks peace is a moral issue. But determining the specific policies necessary to achieve that goal is beyond religion's reach.

The Utopian Dilemma

A utopian strain characterizes Jewish thought and behavior. Abraham Cronbach, professor of social relations at Hebrew Union College for many years, was fond of saying that "whatever inside of any Jewish soul is good and right and holy and noble—that is itself Jewish." Since for Cronbach social justice was "good and right and holy and noble," it followed that "social justice is Jewish."[9]

Few groups in American life have been as willing to set aside their group interests on behalf of what they deem to be the public good. Writing more than twenty years ago, political scientists Edward C. Banfield and James Q. Wilson pondered this atypical behavior and concluded that the Jewish "political ethos is such that a politics of ethnic appeal strikes them . . . as uninteresting and even immoral." The utopian dilemma stems from the fact that for almost a generation now a number of important Jewish interests, along with positions taken by traditional friends or allies, have often come into collision with this ethos. Moreover, traditional strategies they have employed to achieve their public policy goals, however useful these have been in the past, no longer adequately fit the circumstances of American life in the 1980s.

One way in which this utopianism has been expressed is to substitute an ardent desire for peace and social justice for practical ways to advance these desirable goals. Concern for the poor and disadvantaged in society stirs deep emotions and memories, but that compassion is not enough. The formulas of the welfare state developed in the 1930s and 1940s are no longer adequate to the urban problems today. The romanticism that frequently characterizes Jewish public policy formulations finds its purest expression in the notion—the dangerous notion—espoused by several of the religious bodies that we should "reduce our defense expenditures" and cut off military and other forms of support for our admittedly imperfect friends in Central America who are under pressure from the Soviet Union and Cuba as well as indigenous revolutionary forces, in order to deal "with the crisis of our cities and with world-wide problems of poverty." They have focused a great deal of their energy in pressing for the separation of church and state without recognizing that this is both impossible and, often, in terms of self-interest and that of the broader society, undesirable. As Pastor Richard John Neuhaus has noted in his book *The Naked Public Square* published in 1984, "we need to look for quite unprecedented ways of relating politics and religion. . . . The question is whether we can devise forms for that intervention which can revive rather than destroy the liberal democracy that is required by a society that would be pluralistic and free."

The failure of Jewish civic and religious leadership to move away from older public policy formations is unfortunate in a broader sense. It has not been as movers and shakers in the corporate or military power centers but in the world of ideas that Jews have played out their significant role in American life. One recalls how Jewish intellectuals, socialists, and labor leaders helped think through and erect the necessary social supports and government services in the period of unfettered capitalism, and how Jewish community relations agencies broadened America's understanding of the nature of American pluralism and importance of civil liberties safeguards. Jewish groups today have been unable, most especially, to integrate into their thought and social strategies the concept that economic growth is probably the new frontier of civil rights in the 1980s and beyond; that urban enterprise zones, for example, backed by liberal Congressmen Robert Garcia (D., N.Y.) and William Gray (D., Pa.) as well as conservatives like Congressman Jack Kemp (R., N.Y.), are worthy of serious exploration. In their heavy reliance on the welfare state, Jewish leaders have tended to ignore the role of the intermediate institutions such as church, neighborhood, religious, and ethnic groups in undergirding family life with the help of government in dealing with social and economic problems. Too often, Jewish groups have sought easy formulas for Jewish public policy positions in place of hard and rigorous thought, oblivious to the insight that the man of faith is a "utopian without illusion, and a realist with vision."[10]

Most often their utopianism has found expression in older formulas of political liberalism. Jews remain the most liberal of all white groups in the United States. They are disproportionately so on issues involving civil liberties and women. And more so than other white Americans, they support unpopular and non-productive approaches to helping the disadvantaged and minorities. Although relatively affluent and therefore seldom in need of government assistance, they continue to oppose cuts in welfare and in other programs for the poor and to support the New Deal program that found favor with their parents' generation.

One of the most fascinating aspects of contemporary Jewish liberalism has been its constancy despite great changes in society as a whole as well as in the social and economic class of Jews themselves. When most Jews were immigrant workers and small businessmen, they supported socialists. Then, as "a rising but economically insecure middle class," they aligned themselves with Franklin D. Roosevelt and the New Deal. After World War II, as part of the "new class" of highly educated professionals, they helped to build the reform wing of the Democratic Party and the liberal-Left critique of American society. "Far from undermining liberal commitments," Steven M. Cohen writes, "Jews' changing class character has, in fact, harmonized with liberalism's changing style and content in recent decades." A central element here is that Jews' "abiding sense of insecurity" and "partial exclusion until recently from the social mainstream" have resulted in perennial support for liberalism and the Democratic Party. Indeed, their liberalism "should be seen as a reflection (if not, sometimes a strategy) of the entry and integration of Jews into modern society."[11]

Although liberalism continues to be the principal political philosophy of Jews, along with a commitment to Israel, it is nevertheless a somewhat chastened liberalism that reflects the buffeting endured over the past decade. This liberalism has been nourished more by nostalgia for its immigrant-oriented past than by the passion so evident in the Golden Age of American Jewry after World War II. American Judaism has found it difficult to absorb the enormous social and economic changes that have occurred in recent years, or to formulate a new philosophic response.

The semantics of public policy discussion within the Jewish community are a further barrier to creative thought. Issues continue to be debated from either a "liberal" or "conservative" perspective, although these terms have lost much of their meaning. Any attempt to reexamine earlier beliefs and past policies tends to be dismissed by many Jews as a move to the "Right" and therefore "reactionary." Jews have a terrible fear of being seen as "conservative," which they associate with being less humane and less compassionate than they once were. Milton Himmelfarb is fond of saying that when the Jewish arm reaches up to pull the Republican lever, it becomes paralyzed. (He adds, facetiously, that they have incomes like Episcopalians but vote like Puerto Ricans.) The Jewish tendency is to fall back on earlier beliefs and behavior, even when there are growing doubts about their adequacy. Thus, Jewish utopianism can still be periodically ignited, as it was by Jonathan Schell's call to remake the world to avoid nuclear conflagration.

Jews and Power

At the core of this problem is what can only be termed the ambivalent relationship of Jews to power. Forced to live throughout much of their history as a subject people, Jews have made of powerlessness something of a virtue, a means of bringing about the Messianic Era. This tradition has deep emotional and religious roots. "Power buries those who wield it," the Talmud says in discussing the fall of the Roman Empire.[12] Rabbi Richard Rubenstein has criticized the Jewish tendency to oppose exclusionary social patterns in the United States as if they were moral issues alone and to forget that "no group willingly surrenders power to a rival community."[13]

The fact is, the greatest tragedies that have befallen Jews have stemmed from their powerlessness. Yet it would appear that this is still imperfectly understood by Jews. Whether the goal is to resolve the social and economic problems of decaying U.S. cities, maintain the steadily contracting area of political freedom in the world, or avert nuclear catastrophe, Jewish groups, in the main, continue to prefer nursing a utopian idealism to facing harsh realities.

By holding aloft a flag of hope in moments of despair, it is true, Jews have been a source of inspiration and renewal for many. In her diary, Anne Frank wrote that "if we bear all this suffering and there are still Jews left when it is over, then Jews . . . will be held up as an example. Who knows, it might even be our religion from which the world and all people learn good. . . ."[14] One must respect the idealism of this young girl while recalling her fate with sadness. Reform Judaism has probably carried utopianism to its farthest extreme. To its credit, however, Reform has refused to withdraw from the political arena in a period when other Jews have tended to turn inward.

New Jewish Thought

There is good reason to believe that Jewish thought and behavior are taking new directions. The great majority of American Jews today were born in the United States, and they have worked out the "tensions of acculturation." The Holocaust, the realization that the Soviet Union is almost as hostile to Jews as the Nazis were, the perversion of some of the goals and methods of the U.S. civil rights revolution, the decline of many cities, and the growth of a "new paganism" have all had the effect of forcing many Jews to study the uses of power, virtually for the first time.

A large number of Jewish intellectuals, including but hardly limited to Nathan Glazer, Norman Podhoretz, Midge Decter, and Irving Kristol, have played key roles in analyzing political power and how it is used. Although they came to maturity in the 1950s and adopted a universalist, liberal-Left politics, many of these later rediscovered certain dangers Jews faced. By 1972, Podhoretz was suggesting that Jews judge social policies on the basis of the question, "Is it good for the Jews?" Many of these Jewish intellectuals have argued in recent years for a stronger national defense and more support for friendly regimes abroad, and have questioned the growth of the welfare state. A measure of the distance some have traveled is evident in the title of one of Kristol's books, *Two Cheers For Capitalism*. Several journals of opinion, such as *Commentary* (edited by Podhoretz), *The Public Interest* (edited by Kristol and Glazer) and, to some degree, *The New Republic* (whose editor-in-chief and president is Martin Peretz) have also participated in the revaluation of liberalism. Peretz's break with the Left occurred following the Six-Day War, when he wrote that leftist views of Israel brought

> a welcome end of innocence in many other radicals who will from now on be somewhat more skeptical of all nostrums of the *engagés* which have been so readily and thoughtlessly accepted as the desperation bred by the [Viet Nam] war and the riots in our cities intensifies. . . . I suppose that if I'd been wiser and had known more about history—if by that time I had really integrated the long Jewish view of history into my life—I might not have made such mistakes.[15]

These writers and publications, sometimes called "neo-conservative," are having an important impact on national policies. In addition, a group of highly committed and observant Jews devoted to public affairs has emerged, including Daniel J. Elazar, Charles Liebman, and

Leon Jick. While these men are not as visible to the non-Jewish public as the neo-conservatives, they do possess some influence within Jewish circles.

Finally, as Shoshana Bryen has recently suggested, the growth of "new wave" industries grounded in computers and other high technology has brought forward a group of Jews who differ from the post–World War II "new class." Unlike the latter, who have been often linked to liberal and left-wing politics, this group is involved in developing new national security strategies and designing weapons systems for the United States, NATO allies, and friendly nations, including Israel. A highly entrepreneurial group, they believe strongly in preserving and strengthening free enterprise and, in fact, see national revolutions around the world as aimed as much at toppling the middle class as the "ruling classes." As a result, they have shed old stereotypes that have linked military power with anti-Semitic governments. The significance of this "new wave," Bryen says, may be in "its ability to use . . . American and Jewish experiences to formulate a uniquely and consistently 'Jewish position' on issues and events of the 1980s and beyond."[16]

Admittedly, little of this intellectual revaluation of liberalism has shown up in the positions taken by the major Jewish civic agencies. This is not hard to understand. Jewish civic life tends to be an upper-class activity, and those who run the organizations have more time to devote to it than less well-to-do Jews. There are some indications of a shift in opinion among the religious bodies, however, at least in mood. Within Reform Judaism, for example, one finds greater soberness in viewing some of the issues of today. "We have not changed our mode of addressing them," Rabbi Saperstein declares, "but there is greater recognition of their complexity." One indication of this, he suggests, is that Reform's support of the nuclear freeze movement, while strong, does not have the intensity that characterized opposition to the war in Viet Nam.

Similarly, the small but historically influential Reconstructionist movement (whose roots are in Conservative Judaism but which has remained closer to Reform Judaism in its public policy formulations) has begun to ask some hard questions. In a 1983 issue of the *Reconstructionist* devoted entirely to "Reconstructionism and Public Policy," Daniel Nussbaum argued that the times call for social and economic experimentation. "Our own traditions, as well as our present understanding of institutions, suggest that whatever new policies emerge will reflect new arrangements of cooperation and coordination between the public and private sectors. . . ." But after venturing out from the protective circle of liberal orthodoxy, Nussbaum quickly adds that it is necessary for "the public sector to bear the ultimate responsibility for ensuring the welfare of all our citizens."[17]

In the same issue of the *Reconstructionist,* Richard Hirsh pays homage to the principle of separation of church and state, but adds that children in public schools are being exposed to "a non-religious, secular approach to life." It is all well and good to advise parents to recite prayers at home and send their children to church or synagogue, he declares, but the public schools remain the major influence in children's lives. "We are disappointed," he writes, "that Jewish spokesmen have not grappled with the central issue, and have concentrated their attention upon the negative issue of 'separation.' " Concerned that Jews have sided with "atheists and secularists," he urges that readings, songs, and prayers in celebration of American holidays—in short, an American civil religion—be substituted for the banned Bible-reading and prayer.

Hirsh's concern was echoed in a recent issue of *Congress Monthly,* an organ of the militantly liberal American Jewish Congress. In an article called "Church-State Issues: Is the Jewish Community Overreacting?," Marc Stern, an official of the AJCongress, takes civil libertarian groups to task for filing new cases without "any real increase in the number of [church-state] violations." "Should not . . . the Jewish community support legislation to permit student-initiated religious clubs in the public high schools?" he asks, as long as there are safeguards against official participation? He urges the Jewish Left "to ease toward the center by pressing counseling organizations that offer contraceptives and abortion to teach sexual responsibility as well" in order to head off "the growing and alarming rate of teenage pregnancies." In another article, "Must Morality Be Sacrificed to Protect Civil Liberties?," Professor Edward M. Levine of Loyola University argues forcefully that Jewish liberals have not addressed themselves to the "morally corrosive aspects of contemporary society."[18]

Another significant development has been the renewed interest in ritual and tradition across the broad spectrum of American Jewish life. This is reflected in the greater observance of dietary laws at secular

Jewish gatherings, the interest in Jewish studies on college and university campuses by young Jews from non-religious backgrounds, and the rise of religious Orthodoxy, both in numbers and in participation in public affairs.[19] Orthodox Jews no longer hesitate to get into politics at the grass roots. They have opposed busing and abortion on demand. Many have little sympathy for a nuclear freeze or cuts in the U.S. defense budget. They have become familiar figures in state capitals, at congressional hearings, and at the White House, especially because of their efforts to obtain public aid for their religious schools. But despite its growth and dynamism, Orthodoxy has been hampered by its strain of fanaticism, by its fundamentally separatist ideology, and by its inability to reach more than a small segment of the American-born Jewish population.

Perhaps the most interesting group to watch is Conservative Judaism, the largest of the Jewish religious bodies. Conservative Judaism's goal down through the years has been to mediate between tradition and modernity without losing authenticity. The positions it takes on public policy issues—and even its silences—are highly significant. The decision of the Rabbinical Assembly to come out in favor of tuition tax credits was an important shift. And even though other elements of the Conservative movement have been pro-choice, the assembly has declined to speak out in favor of abortion on demand. On the other hand, the decision of the faculty of the Jewish Theological Seminary in 1983 to ordain women suggests that Conservative Judaism remains a centrist movement.

Although liberalism "has constituted American Jews' principal political response to the opportunity to integrate into the large society," there is a difference in how various Jewish groups respond to it. More "segregated, more traditionally oriented Jews tend to report lower levels of political liberalism," while the most secularized and thoroughly assimilated Jews tend to line up in the political center. The third group—"those who affirmatively but marginally identify as Jews"—comprises the most liberal in politics.[20]

Impact on Behavior

The newer currents now flowing in the Jewish community have begun to seep into political behavior. Democratic presidential candidates have normally received a high percentage of the Jewish vote, but this was reduced to 65 per cent in 1972, revived somewhat to 72 per cent in 1976, and then dropped precipitously to 45 per cent in 1980.

In the 1984 election, the *New York Times*–CBS News, *Washington Post*–ABC News, and NBC News polls showed that the Jewish vote for Reagan was somewhere between 31 and 35 per cent. This has been disputed, however, by the conservative National Jewish Coalition, which claims that its more detailed polling indicated the figure to be nearer to 40 per cent or better. The non-partisan Jewish Community Relations Council in New York City reported that some 38 per cent of Jews in the city supported the President, an increase of 2 per cent over 1980.[21] However one seeks to resolve this dispute over the figures, the fact remains that in national elections since 1972, the Watergate year of 1976 excepted, it appears that between one out of three and two out of five Jewish voters have brought themselves to pull the Republican lever. Moreover, a high proportion of Jewish voters today clearly identify with moderate Democrats rather than with the party's left wing, as represented by George McGovern and Jesse Jackson.

This is not a trivial shift. Jews, it is true, continue to feel liberal, but a significant number of them have concluded that different voting behavior is not only permitted but needed. "Probably the most important reason for this change," Himmelfarb suggests, is "the desire for a strong, resolute America and a secure Israel."[22]

These new trends have been bolstered by the stepped-up activities of the National Jewish Coalition led by Richard J. Fox of Philadelphia and a vigorous group of younger and generally more affluent Jewish leaders. From a handful of people at the start of the 1984 campaign, it has grown in numbers and outreach, and doubtless will make an even stronger push in 1988 on behalf of the Republican national ticket. Its problem, as Deborah Lipstadt, Charles Pruitt, and Jonathan Woocher recently pointed out, is "that there is still a considerable gap between identifying as a conservative and identifying as a Republican."[23]

Throughout much of their recent history, American Jews have been torn between universalism and particularism. Under universalism they helped shape the "good society," in which they saw the fulfillment of Judaism's prophetic ideals. Those drawn to particularism, on the other hand, have argued that as a small and historically detested minority, Jews must frame their public policy positions on the basis of self-interest. "Is it good or bad for the Jews?" is the half-mocking, half-serious question they like to ask themselves. In the United States, where Jews have experienced many difficulties but achieved some success and greater acceptance, universalism has been the dominant mode of thought and behavior. The events of recent decades, however, have sharply shaken the faith and optimism upon which Jewish universalism is based. In his 1978 book *Reform Judaism Today,* Eugene Borowitz wondered whether "the giddiness which resulted from the breathtaking advancement of Jews, and the anxiety that Jews might lose their rights because they were thought to be interested only in themselves, explain what seems to us their overemphasis on existing to serve others."[24] Despite the setbacks, he urged Jews not to give up on universal hopes. What seems to be finally emerging is a better balance between universalism and particularism. If this is a valid conclusion, it cannot help being "good for the Jews" and good for the broader society of which they are a part.

Notes

Chapter One

1. Henry Feingold, "Courage First and Intelligence Second: The American Jewish Secular Elite, Roosevelt and the Failure to Rescue," *American Jewish History,* June 1983, p. 425.
2. Charles S. Liebman, *The Ambivalent American Jew: Politics, Religion and Family in American Jewish Life* (Philadelphia, Pa.: Jewish Publication Society of America, 1973), pp. 75-76.
3. Seymour N. Siegel et al., *Who Speaks for American Judaism?* (Washington, D.C.: Ethics and Public Policy Center, 1983).
4. See, for example, Stephen D. Isaacs, *Jews and American Politics* (Garden City, N.Y.: Doubleday and Co., 1974), pp. 148-49.
5. Steven M. Cohen, "The 1981-82 National Survey of American Jews," *American Jewish Year Book, 1983* (New York and Philadelphia: The American Jewish Committee and The Jewish Publication Society of America, 1982), p. 102; see also Steven M. Cohen, *American Modernity and Jewish Identity* (New York: Tavistock Publications, 1983), p. 143.
6. Isaiah 1: 17 and 21.
7. David Saperstein, "The Talmud and the College Loan Program, Etc.," *Moment,* July-August 1982, pp. 56-63; also see Adam Simms, "Economic Justice: The Jewish Tradition," a paper prepared for the American Jewish Committee for presentation to an Interfaith Dialogue on Economic Justice, 17 April 1983.
8. Sarah Bershtel and Allen Graubard, "The Mystique of the Progressive Jew," *Working Papers,* March-April 1983, p. 21.
9. Liebman, *The Ambivalent American Jew,* p. 142.
10. Werner Cohn as quoted in Chaim I. Waxman, "The Fourth Generation Grows Up: The Contemporary Jewish Community," in *Annals of the American Academy of Political and Social Science,* March 1981, p. 111.
11. Liebman, *The Ambivalent American Jew,* p. 150.
12. See Frederic V. Grunfeld, *Prophets Without Honor: A Background to Freud, Kafka, Einstein, and Their World* (New York: Holt, Rinehart and Winston, 1979), p. 38.
13. Hasia R. Diner, *In the Almost Promised Land: American Jews and Blacks, 1915-1935* (Westport, Conn.: Greenwood Press, 1977), p. xiii.
14. Cohen, *American Modernity and Jewish Identity,* p. 136.
15. Siegel et al., *Who Speaks for American Judaism?,* pp. 12-14.
16. As quoted in Deborah Dash Moore, *At Home in America: Second Generation New York Jews* (New York: Columbia University Press, 1981), p. 228.
17. Henry L. Feingold, *A Midrash on American Jewish History* (Albany, N.Y.: State University of New York Press, 1982), p. 198.

18. For fuller discussion, see Irving Howe, *World of Our Fathers* (New York: Harcourt Brace Jovanovich, 1976), pp. 102-8.
19. Joseph Epstein, "The Education of an Anti-Capitalist," *Commentary*, August 1983, p. 54.
20. As quoted in Lenora E. Berson, *The Negroes and the Jews* (New York: Random House, 1971), p. 109.
21. Philip Scharper, *Torah and Gospel: Jewish and Catholic Theology in Dialogue* (New York: Sheed and Ward, 1966), p. 184.
22. Abba Hillel Silver, *Where Judaism Differed* (New York: The Macmillan Co., 1956), p. 152.
23. W. Gunther Plaut, *The Growth of Reform Judaism* (New York: World Union for Progressive Judaism, 1965), p. 118.
24. As quoted in Eugene B. Borowitz, *Reform Judaism Today: How We Live* (New York: Behrman House, 1978), p. 34.
25. Leonard J. Mervis, "The Social Justice Movement and the American Reform Rabbi," *American Jewish Archives*, June 1955, pp. 172-74.
26. Arthur Gilbert, *A Jew in Christian America* (New York: Sheed and Ward, 1966), pp. 95-96.
27. Mervis, "The Social Justice Movement," p. 172.
28. Mervis, "The Social Justice Movement," p. 178; Gilbert, *A Jew in Christian America*, p. 83.
29. Mervis, "The Social Justice Movement," p. 182.
30. Gilbert, *A Jew in Christian America*, p. 89.
31. Ibid., p. 80.
32. Elliot Stevens and Simeon Glaser, *Resolutions Passed by the Central Conference of American Rabbis, 1889-1974* (hereafter *CCAR Resolutions*), rev. ed. (New York: 1975), p. 64.
33. Henry L. Feingold, *Zion in America*, rev. ed. (New York: Hippocrene Books, Inc., 1981), p. 166.
34. Gilbert, *A Jew in Christian America*, p. 89.
35. Max J. Routtenberg, "Seventy-Five Years of Changing Concern, Emphasis and Philosophy," Proceedings of the Rabbinical Assembly of America, vol. 37 (1975), p. 305.
36. Albert Vorspan and Eugene Lipman, *Justice and Judaism: The Work of Social Action* (New York: Union of American Hebrew Congregations, 1956), p. 305.
37. Louis Bernstein, *Challenge and Mission: The Emergence of the English-Speaking Orthodox Rabbinate* (New York: Sheingold Publishers, Inc., 1982), p. 13.
38. As quoted in Howe, *World of Our Fathers*, p. 199.
39. Bernard J. Bamberger, *The Synagogue Council of America, A Brief History* (New York: Synagogue Council of America Publications, 1963), p. 2.
40. Ibid.
41. Ibid.

Chapter Two

1. NJCRAC Joint Program Plan, 1964-65, pp. 3-10
2. Abraham J. Karp, *A History of the United Synagogue, 1913-1963* (New York: United Synagogue of America, 1964), p. 81; Liebman, *The Ambivalent American Jew*, pp. 60-61.

3. As quoted by Gail Naron Chalew.
4. Liebman, *The Ambivalent American Jew*, pp. 75-76.
5. Karp, *A History of the United Synagogue*, p. 72.
6. Bamberger, *The Synagogue Council of America*, p. 7.
7. Stevens and Glaser, *CCAR Resolutions*, p. 71.
8. Stevens and Glaser, *CCAR Resolutions*, p. 26; *Where We Stand*, Social Action Resolutions Adopted by the Union of American Hebrew Congregations, rev. ed. (UAHC Commission on Social Action of Reform Judaism, 1980), p. 33.
9. United Synagogue Council of America resolution, 1955.
10. Feingold, *Zion in America*, p. 319.
11. Stevens and Glaser, *CCAR Resolutions*, p. 48.
12. Liebman, The *Ambivalent American Jew*, p. 67; Lucy S. Dawidowicz, *The Jewish Presence: Essays on Identity and History* (New York: Holt, Rinehart and Winston, 1976), p. 86.
13. Vorspan and Lipman, *Justice and Judaism*, p. 198.
14. Ibid., p. 185.
15. Ibid., pp. 186-90.
16. Murray Friedman, "Economic Growth and Civil Rights," *Journal of Contemporary Studies*, Winter 1981, pp. 51-57.
17. NJCRAC Joint Program Plan, 1953-54, p. 3.
18. Kenneth B. Clark, *Prejudice and Your Child*, 2nd ed. (Boston, Mass.: Beacon Press, 1963), dedication and p. x.
19. James Q. Wilson, *Negro Politics: The Search for Leadership* (Glencoe, Ill.: Free Press, 1960), p. 149.
20. Chaim I. Waxman, *America's Jews in Transition* (Philadelphia, Pa.: Temple University Press, 1983), p. 105.
21. Bershtel and Graubard, "Mystique of the Progressive Jew," p. 21.
22. James A. Sleeper and Alan J. Mintz, *The New Jews* (New York: Vintage Books, 1971), pp. 13-14.
23. Bernstein, *Challenge and Mission*, p. 185.
24. Stevens and Glaser, *CCAR Resolutions*, pp. 118-26.
25. Karp, *A History of the United Synagogue*, p. 93.
26. For further discussion of the role of Southern rabbis, see P. Allen Krause, "Rabbis and Negro Rights in the South, 1954-1967," *American Jewish Archives*, 21: 1 (April 1969).
27. Statement by Henry Siegman of the Synagogue Council of America, 13 March 1968.
28. Mathew Ahmann, ed., *Race: Challenge to Religion* (Chicago, Ill.: Henry Regnery Co., 1963), p. v.
29. Samuel H. Dresner, "The Contribution of Abraham Joshua Heschel," *Judaism*, Winter 1983, pp. 57-58.
30. Hillel Goldberg, "Abraham Joshua Heschel and His Times," *Midstream*, April 1982, p. 37.
31. Abraham J. Heschel, *The Insecurity of Freedom: Essays on Human Existence* (New York: Noonday Press, 1967), p. 85.
32. Ibid., pp. 97-98.
33. Jack Riemer, "Abraham Joshua Heschel," *Present Tense*, Summer 1983, pp. 39-42.
34. Scharper, *Torah and Gospel*, p. 199.

35. Ibid., p. 201.
36. Routtenberg, "Seventy-Five Years of Changing Concern," p. 305.
37. Albert Vorspan, *Jewish Values and Social Crisis: A Casebook for Social Action* (New York: Union of American Hebrew Congregations, 1968), pp. 118-19. See appendix, "Why We Went."
38. Charles S. Liebman, "Orthodoxy in American Jewish Life," in Marshall Sklare, *The Jewish Community in American Life* (New York: Berman House, 1974), p. 138.
39. "The War on Poverty," *CCAR Yearbook*, 1965, p. 71.
40. Arthur Hertzberg, *Being Jewish in America: The Modern Experience* (New York: Schocken Books, 1979), p. 156.
41. Bernstein, *Challenge and Mission*, p. 157
42. Bamberger, *The Synagogue Council of America*, p. 5.
43. Frank Sorauf, *The Wall of Separation* (Princeton, N.J.: Princeton University Press, 1976), p. 161.
44. Terry Eastland, "In Defense of Religious America," *Commentary*, June 1981.
45. Egon Mayer, *From Suburb to Shtetel: The Jews of Boro Park* (Philadelphia, Pa.: Temple University Press, 1979), pp. 8-11 and pp. 123-25; also see William B. Helmreich, *The World of the Yeshiva: An Intimate Portrait of Orthodox Jewry* (New York: Macmillan, The Free Press, 1982).
46. Background Papers in Jewish Education, American Jewish Committee, "Jewish Education: Who, What, How," May 1983, p. 4.
47. *The Struggle and the Splendor: Pictorial Overview of Agudath Israel of America* (New York: Agudath Israel of America, 1982), p. 107.
48. NJCRAC Joint Program Plan, 1962-63, p. 7; Liebman, "Orthodoxy in American Jewish Life," p. 148.
49. Nathaniel Weyl, *The Jew in American Politics* (New Rochelle, N.Y.: Arlington House, 1968), p. 317.
50. Ibid., p. 323.
51. Gilbert, *A Jew in Christian America*, p. 147.
52. Gilbert, *A Jew in Christian America*, p. 150; Agudath Israel, *The Struggle and the Splendor*, p. 107.
53. NJCRAC Joint Program Plan, 1965-66, pp. 14-16.
54. Gilbert, *A Jew in Christian America*, p. 154.
55. Mayer, *From Suburb to Shtetel*, pp. 130, 174.
56. Isaacs, *Jews and American Politics*, p. 20.

CHAPTER THREE

1. Kerner Commission, *Report of the National Advisory Commission on Civil Disorders* (New York: Bantam Books, 1968), p.1.
2. "Despite charges of sharp practices, the merchants of the Columbia area (in Philadelphia) are not making inordinate profits," wrote Lenora Berson in *Case Study of a Riot: The Philadelphia Story* (New York: Institute of Human Relations Press, 1966), p. 45. Also see Murray Friedman's discussion of this point in: Peter Rose, Stanley Rothman, and William J. Wilson, eds., *Through Different Eyes: Black and White Perspectives on American Race Relations* (New York: Oxford University Press, 1973), pp. 151-52.
3. Friedman, in Rose, Rothman, Wilson, *Through Different Eyes*, p. 155.

4. Hyman Bookbinder, "Remembering Dr. King," *The Jewish Week*, Washington, D.C., 25 August 1983.
5. Robert G. Weisbord and Arthur Stein, *Bitter Sweet Encounter* (Westport, Conn.: University Press, 1970), p. 139.
6. NJCRAC Joint Program Plan, 1960-61, p. 51.
7. United Synagogue Council of America resolution, 1969.
8. Weisbord and Stein, *Bitter Sweet Encounter*, p. 157.
9. Friedman, in Rose, Rothman, Wilson, *Through Different Eyes*, p. 148.
10. As quoted in Murray Friedman, "Religion and Politics in an Age of Pluralism, 1945-1976," *Publius*, Summer 1980, p. 55.
11. Peter Schrag, *The Decline of the WASP* (New York: Simon and Schuster, 1970), pp. 76-77.
12. Julius Weinberg, "The Trouble with Reform Judaism," *Commentary*, November 1979, p. 54.
13. Albert Vorspan, *To Do Justly* (New York: Union of American Hebrew Congregations, 1969), p. 65.
14. Henry Cohen, *Justice, Justice* (New York: Union of American Hebrew Congregations, 1968), p. 121.
15. NJCRAC Joint Program Plan, 1968-69, p. 7.
16. Vorspan, *Jewish Values and Social Crisis*, p. 66.
17. Cohen, *Justice, Justice*, p. 112.
18. Ibid., p. 118.
19. Vorspan, *Jewish Values and Social Crisis*, p. 67.
20. Ibid., p. 61.
21. Rabbinical Assembly Congressional Proceedings, 1968, p. 251.
22. NJCRAC Joint Program Plan, 1969-70, p. 18.
23. Berson, *Case Study of a Riot*, p. 6.
24. Vorspan, *To Do Justly*, pp. 63-64.
25. Claybourne Carson, Jr., "Blacks and Jews in the Civil Rights Movement," in Joseph R. Washington, *Jews in Black Perspectives: A Dialogue* (New Jersey: Fairleigh Dickinson Press, 1984), p. 118.
26. Waxman, *America's Jews in Transition*, p. 105.
27. Arthur I. Waskow, *The Freedom Seder: A New Haggadah for Passover* (Washington, D.C.: Micah Press, 1969), p. 45.
28. Arthur I. Waskow, *The Bush Is Burning! Radical Judaism Faces the Pharaohs of the Modern Superstate* (New York: The Macmillan Co., 1971), pp. 7-20; Waskow, *The Freedom Seder*, p. v., pp. 42-45.
29. NJCRAC Joint Program Plan, 1975-76, p. 30; 1977-78, p. 31.
30. United Synagogue Council of America resolution, 11 October 1972.
31. *American Jewish Year Book*, 1970, p. 332.
32. Daniel P. Moynihan, *The Politics of a Guaranteed Income: The Nixon Administration and the Family Assistance Plan* (New York: Vintage Books, 1973), pp. 299-302.
33. See, for example, Earl Raab, "The Black Revolution and the Jewish Question," *Commentary*, January 1969, p. 30.
34. NJCRAC Joint Program Plan, 1974-75, p. 36.
35. Ibid., p. 40.
36. Ibid., p. 32.
37. NJCRAC Joint Program Plan, 1972-73, p. 30; 1975-76, p. 34; 1978-79, p. 39.
38. P. 51.

39. Friedman, in Rose, Rothman, Wilson, *Through Different Eyes*, p. 160.
40. Isaacs, *Jews and American Politics*, pp. 165-74.
41. Hertzberg, *Being Jewish in America*, p. 183.
42. Ibid., pp. 180-90.
43. NJCRAC Joint Program Plan, 1970-71, p. 41.
44. NJCRAC Joint Program Plan, 1977-78, p. 10; 1978-79, p. 22.
45. Stevens and Glaser, *CCAR Resolutions*, p. 74.
46. Weyl, *The Jew in American Politics*, p. 168.
47. Vorspan, *Casebook*, pp. 13-15.
48. *American Jewish Year Book*, 1967, p. 8.
49. Stephen B. Oates, *Let the Trumpet Sound: The Life of Martin Luther King, Jr.* (New York: Harper and Row, 1982), p. 433.
50. Waskow, *The Bush Is Burning*, p. 23.
51. *American Jewish Year Book*, 1967, pp. 79-80.
52. Interview with Rabbi Balfour Brickner, *Village Voice*, 7 September 1982; 28 January 1983.
53. Vorspan, *To Do Justly*, p. 66.
54. Stevens and Glaser, *CCAR Resolutions*, p. 72.
55. *American Jewish Year Book*, 1969, p. 255.
56. Richard Rubenstein, "The Politics of Powerlessness," *Reconstructionist*, 17 May 1968, pp. 7-15.
57. Isaacs, *Jews and American Politics*, p. 148.
58. Symposium at seventieth anniversary of the Rabbinical Assembly, 1970, pp. 86-139.
59. Ibid., p. 126.
60. Feingold, *Zion in America*, p. 161.
61. Borowitz, *Reform Judaism Today*, p. xxiv.
62. Goldberg, "Abraham Joshua Heschel and His Times," p. 41.

Chapter Four

1. Irving M. Kristol, "What's Wrong With NATO?," *New York Times Magazine*, 25 September 1983, pp. 64-71.
2. Charles Silberman, "Crime and Punishment," *The New Republic*, 6 December 1983, p. 7.
3. "March to Nowhere," *The New Republic*, 9 and 26 September 1983, p. 10.
4. See, for example, Jack A. Meyer, ed., *Meeting Human Needs: Toward a New Public Philosophy* (Washington, D.C.: American Enterprise Institute, 1982).
5. Peter Berger and Richard John Neuhaus, *To Empower People: The Role of Mediating Structures in Public Policy* (Washington, D.C.: American Enterprise Institute, 1977).
6. Walter Williams, *The State Against Blacks* (New York: McGraw-Hill, 1982), pp. 39-44.
7. As quoted in Howard Banks and Jayne A. Pearl, "Poverty in America," *Forbes*, 29 August 1983, pp. 39-41.
8. Irving M. Kristol, *Two Cheers for Capitalism* (New York: Basic Books, 1978); Michael Novak, *The Spirit of Democratic Capitalism* (New York: Simon and Schuster, 1982); and Paul Johnson, *Modern Times: The World From the Twenties to the Eighties* (New York: Harper and Row, 1983).

9. Murray Friedman, *New Perspectives in School Integration* (Philadelphia, Pa.: Fortress Press, 1979), pp. 23-31.

10. Ibid., pp. 111-23.

11. Eugene P. McManus, "The Catholic School and Education Within the Black Community," supplement to *Catholic League Newsletter* 9:2, no date.

12. James S. Coleman, Thomas Hoffer, and Sally Kilgore, *High School Achievement: Public, Catholic, and Parochial Schools Compared* (New York: Basic Books, 1982).

13. James Q. Wilson, "Crime and American Culture," *The Public Interest*, Winter 1983, p. 36; see also his *Thinking About Crime* (New York: Basic Books, 1975).

14. *Philadelphia Inquirer*, 11 September 1982.

15. *American Jewish Year Book*, 1977, p. 141.

16. NJCRAC Joint Program Plan, 1978-79, p. 36.

17. *New York Times*, 13 September 1983.

18. Speech by Albert Vorspan, 2 September 1982, High Holy Days Leadership Conference in New York, sponsored by the Synagogue Council of America and the World Jewish Congress.

19. George Will, *Philadelphia Inquirer*, 23 August 1983.

20. Eugene B. Borowitz, "Liberalism and the Jews," *Commentary*, January 1980, p. 24.

21. *American Jewish Year Book*, 1981, pp. 125-27; Murray Friedman, "Black Anti-Semitism on the Rise," *Commentary*, October 1979, pp. 31-35.

22. Speech by Albert Vorspan, Jewish Telegraphic Agency Daily News Bulletin, 23 February 1984; *Philadelphia Tribune*, 29 November 1983; news release, UAHC, 15 November 1983.

23. *New York Times*, 28 June 1984.

24. *Jewish Exponent*, 9 September 1983.

25. *The New Republic*, 9 and 26 September 1983.

26. *Jewish Exponent*, 29 July 1983.

27. *Philadelphia Tribune*, 13 September 1983.

28. *American Jewish Year Book*, 1982, p. 103.

29. *The Challenge of the Religious Right: A Jewish Response* (Washington, D.C.: Commission on Social Action of Reform Judaism, no date).

30. *American Jewish Year Book*, 1983, p. 669.

31. Ibid., p. 71. *Jewish Exponent* (Philadelphia) March 22, 1985.

32. Jonathan D. Sarna, "Jews, the Moral Majority and American Tradition," *Journal of Reform Judaism*, Spring 1982, pp. 1-8.

33. Burton Yale Pines, "A Majority for Morality," *Public Opinion Quarterly*, April-May 1981.

34. Mark A. Golub, "The Radical Right," statement prepared for the CCAR Justice and Peace Committee, no date.

35. Wolfe Kelman to author, 3 February 1984.

36. Women's League for Conservative Judaism, *Index of World Affairs Resolutions*, March 1979, p. 1.

37. Agudath Israel, *The Struggle and the Splendor*, pp. 142-43.

38. NJCRAC Joint Program Plan, 1975-76, p. 56.

39. "The Abortion Perplexity," *The New Republic*, 11 July 1983.

40. *Philadelphia Inquirer*, 11 February 1983.

41. Interview with Balfour Brickner, 28 January 1983.

42. NJCRAC Joint Program Plan, 1982-83, p. 50.

43. Jewish Telegraph Agency News Bulletin, 27 August 1984.
44. "American Holy War," *The New Republic*, 9 April 1984, p. 19.
45. George Will, *Philadelphia Inquirer*, 22 January 1983.
46. Siegel et al., *Who Speaks for American Judaism?*, p. 31.
47. *CCAR Yearbook*, 1976, p. 66.
48. CCAR resolution, 1982; Jewish Telegraphic Agency Daily News Bulletin, 3 June 1983.
49. UAHC resolution, 3 December 1982.
50. *New York Times*, 20 January 1983.
51. *Philadelphia Inquirer*, 2 January 1984.
52. Shoshana Bryen, "The PLO in Central America," *Newsletter* (Jewish Institute for National Security Affairs), June 1983.
53. *Philadelphia Inquirer*, 20 April 1983.
54. As quoted in Ronald Radosh, "Darkening Nicaragua," *The New Republic*, 24 October 1983.
55. George Will, *International Herald Tribune*, 26 July 1983.
56. Grunfeld, *Prophets Without Honor*, p. 183.
57. Vorspan, *Jewish Values and Social Crisis*, pp. 32-41.
58. As quoted in Norman Podhoretz, "Appeasement by Any Other Name," *Commentary*, July 1983, p. 25.
59. Robert E. Kiernan, "Toward a Strategy of Peace," *Newsletter* (Institute for Contemporary Studies), July 1982, p. 6.
60. Kristol, "What's Wrong With NATO?," p. 70.
61. Andrei Sakharov, "The Danger of Thermonuclear War," *Foreign Affairs*, Summer 1983.
62. Speech by Albert Vorspan to High Holy Day Leadership Conference, 2 September 1982.
63. UAHC resolution, 3 December 1981.
64. *Philadelphia Inquirer*, 20 August 1983.
65. Milton Himmelfarb, "Are Jews Becoming Republican?," *Commentary*, August 1981, pp. 27-31.
66. *Jewish Exponent*, 3 December 1982.
67. Synagogue Council of America News, 24 February 1983; Norma Schlager, SCA program director, to author, 16 March 1983.
68. For discussion of the various postures, see Wolf Blitzer, "The Nuclear Freeze as a Jewish Issue," *Hadassah Magazine*, May 1983.
69. *Philadelphia Inquirer*, 22 May 1983.
70. For the view of the French bishops, see *New York Times*, 9 July 1983.
71. As quoted by Robert Jastrow, "Why Strategic Superiority Matters," *Commentary*, March 1983, p. 32.
72. Jewish Telegraphic Agency Daily News Bulletin, 20 April 1983.

Chapter Five

1. As quoted in Borowitz, *Reform Judaism Today*, p. 101.
2. Personal interview with Joshua O. Haberman, 17 November 1982.
3. Ernest W. Lefever, *Amsterdam to Nairobi: The World Council of Churches and the Third World* (Washington, D.C.: Ethics and Public Policy Center, 1979).
4. Avery Dulles, *Washington Times*, 17 November 1982.

5. J. Brian Benestad, *The Pursuit of a Just Social Order: Policy Statements of the U.S. Catholic Bishops, 1966-1980* (Washington, D.C.: Ethics and Public Policy Center, 1982).

6. Dawidowicz, *The Jewish Presence*, p. 85.

7. Seymour N. Siegel, "Religion and Social Action," *Proceedings* (Rabbinical Assembly, 1961), pp. 143-63.

8. *The Condition of Jewish Belief* (New York: The Macmillan Co., 1966), p. 130.

9. Abraham Cronbach, "The Essence of American Judaism: A Review Essay," *Modern Judaism*, 32:2 (May 1983), p. 237.

10. Siegel, "Religion and Social Action," p. 155.

11. Steven M. Cohen, *American Modernity and Jewish Identity* (New York: Tavistock Publications, 1983), pp. 136-37.

12. Stanley Rabinowitz, "Yavneh and Bethar: Approaches to Survival," *Newsletter* (Jewish Institute for National Security Affairs), October 1982.

13. Rubenstein, "The Politics of Powerlessness," p. 8.

14. Benno Weiser Varon, "Anne Frank's Voice Uncensored," *Present Tense*, Spring 1983, p. 6.

15. Robert Leiter, "Renaissance Man," *Present Tense*, Winter 1984, p. 19.

16. Shashana Bryen, "The National Defense Outlook in the Jewish Community," *Newsletter* (Jewish Institute for National Security Affairs, May 1984), p. 14.

17. Daniel Nussbaum, "Reconstructionism and Public Policy," *The Reconstructionist*, November-December 1983, p. 15.

18. Edward M. Levine, "Must Morality Be Sacrificed to Protect Civil Liberties?," *The Reconstructionist*, November-December 1983, pp. 5-9.

19. Jonathan D. Sarna, "The Great American Jewish Awakening," *Midstream*, October 1982, pp. 30-34.

20. Cohen, *American Modernity and Jewish Identity*, p. 174.

21. See Long Island *Jewish World*, 16-22 November 1984; Arthur Hertzberg, "Reagan and the Jews," *The New York Review of Books*, 31 January 1985, p. 12.

22. Himmelfarb, "Are Jews Becoming Republican?," pp. 30-31.

23. Deborah Lipstadt, Charles Pruitt, and Jonathan Woocher, "Election 84: Where Are the Jews?," *Moment*, October 1984, p. 38.

24. Borowitz, *Reform Judaism Today*, p. 106.

Index of Names

ABC News, 97
Abington Township v. *Schempp,* 30
Abram, Morris B., 46, 55, 69
Abramowitz, Rabbi Mayer, 55-56
Abrams, Elliott, 78-79
"Adeste Fideles," 76
ADL, *see* Anti-Defamation League
Adler, Rabbi Morris, 32
Afghanistan, 58, 78, 82
AFL-CIO, 22
Agudath Harabbonim, 15
Agudath Israel of America, 15, 31-32, 34, 53, 73, 84-86
Agudath Israel World Organization, 15
AIPAC, *see* American Israel Public Affairs Committee
AJC, *see* American Jewish Committee
Akron, Ohio, 73
Alabama, 25
Ali, Muhammad, 38
America, 33
American Civil Liberties Union (ACLU), 74
American Federation of Teachers, 33
American Israel Public Affairs Committee (AIPAC), 10
American Jewish Committee (AJC), 2, 8, 19, 21, 23, 34, 42-43, 45-47, 55, 64, 69, 79
American Jewish Congress, 8-9, 23, 27, 29, 33-34, 42, 51, 95
American Judaism (Glazer), 50
American Scholar, The, 61
Amos, 4
Anderson, John, 3
Anti-Defamation League of B'nai B'rith (ADL), 2, 8, 19-20, 23, 41-42, 47-48, 53, 69, 72
Arab Anti-Defamation League, 70
Arabs, 3, 36, 49-50, 53, 55, 77
Arafat, Yasser, 50, 67
Argentina, 77
Ashkenazim, 11
Auletta, Ken, 58-59
Authoritarian Personality, The, 23
Axis powers, 80

Baeck, Leo S., 19
Bakke v. *University of California,* 46, 68-69
Bamburger, Bernard, 16
Banfield, Edward C., 89
Baptist Joint Committee on Public Affairs, 34, 75
Bell, Derrick A., 61
Benestad, J. Brian, 88
Berger, Peter, 59
Berkeley, California, 27, 44
Bernstein, Blanche, 58
Bernstein, Leonard, 2, 82
Bernstein, Rabbi Philip, 24
Berrigan, Daniel, 44, 52
Berrigan, Philip, 44
Bershtel, Sarah, 4
Bible, 12, 30, 32, 58, 75-76, 95
Birmingham, Alabama, 27
Black Muslims, 68
Black Nationalism, 37
Black Power, 37, 40
B'nai B'rith, 2, 8, 84
Bok, Derek, 84
Bookbinder, Hyman, 47
Borowitz, Eugene B., 55, 66, 98
Boston, 31, 53
Bradley, Thomas, 3
Brickner, Rabbi Balfour, 52, 75
Bronx High School of Science, 43
Bronx, N.Y., 62
Brooklyn, N.Y., 39
Brown, H. Rap, 37
Brown, Tony, 70
Brown v. *Board of Education,* 23
Bryen, Shoshana, 94
Buber, Martin, 19, 44
Bukovsky, Vladimir, 83
Bunche, Ralph, 26

California, 3, 61
Cambodia, 53-54, 77
Carmichael, Stokely, 43
Carter, Jimmy, 3, 54, 58, 64, 77, 81-82
Catholic Church, *see* Roman Catholic Church

INDEX OF NAMES

CBS News, 97
CCAR, *see* Central Conference of American Rabbis
Census Bureau, U.S., 59
Center for Disease Control, 74
Central America, 70, 78, 80, 89
Central Conference of American Rabbis (CCAR), 11-13, 20-22, 25, 27-28, 33, 40, 51-53, 65-67, 69, 77-78, 81, 84
CETA (Comprehensive Employment Training Act), 65
Chasidism, 25, 31, 34
Chicago, 3, 18, 25, 44
Chicago, University of, 60
Chicanos, 39
Chinese, 54
Christianity, 5, 11-12, 17, 29, 42
Christian Right, 71, 75
Christmas, 76
Clark, Kenneth B., 23
Clay, Cassius, 38
Cleaver, Eldridge, 37, 44
Coalition for Better Television, 58
Cohen, Rabbi Henry, 40-41
Cohen, Steven M., 5, 91
Cold War, 21
Coleman, James, 61-62
Commentary, 7, 55, 66, 79, 83, 93
Commission on Civil Rights, U.S., 69
Commission on Law and Social Action, 29
Commission on Social Justice, CCAR, 13
Committee on Jewish Law and Standards, 73
Committee on Justice and Race, CCAR, 40, 71
Communal Affairs Committee, UOJC, 20
Communism, 13, 43, 52, 53, 79
Conference of Jewish Communal Service, 46
Conference of Presidents of Major American Jewish Organizations, 10
Congressional Budget Office, 66
Congress Monthly, 95
Congress of Racial Equality (CORE), 38
Congress, U.S., 22, 27-28, 42, 72
Conservative Judaism, 14-15, 19-20, 22, 25-26, 31, 55, 73, 94, 96
Coons, John, 61
Cornell University, 52
Council of Jewish Federations, 84
Cronbach, Abraham, 11, 89
Cruse, Harold, 37
Cuba, 78-79, 89
Cuomo, Mario, 3

Dallas, Texas, 76
Dawidowicz, Lucy, 88
Declining Significance of Race, The (Wilson), 60
Decter, Midge, 93
De Funis v. *Odegard*, 46
Democratic National Convention (1968), 44
Democratic party, 2-3, 91, 96-97
Detroit, 36, 69
Dickstein, Morris, 39
Diner, Hasia, 5
Dissent, 7
Dulles, Avery, S.J., 88

Economic Opportunity Act of 1964, 28
Egypt, 38, 44, 49
Einstein, Albert, 2, 80
Eisendrath, Rabbi Maurice, 20, 51
Eisenhower, Dwight D., 22
Elazar, Daniel J., 72, 93
Elementary and Secondary Education Act of 1965, 33-34
Elijah, 52
El Salvador, 78-79
Emancipation Proclamation, 25
Emunah Women of America, 79
Encounter, 7
Engel v. *Vitale*, 30
England, 4
Enlightenment, 5
Episcopalians, 92
Epstein, Benjamin, 8
Epstein, Joseph, 7, 61
Equal Rights Amendment (ERA), 40, 48, 58
Etzioni, Amitai, 19
Europe, 7-11, 13, 81-83, 85, 88
Everson v. *Board of Education*, 30
Exodus, 80

Fair Employment Practices Commission, 24-25
Falwell, Jerry, 71-72
Family Assistance Program (FAP), 46
Fanon, Franz, 37
Farrakhan, Louis, 68
Fast Day of Esther, 27
Federal Council of Churches, 12, 17
Federation of Reconstructionist Congregations and Havurot, 64
Feingold, Henry, 1, 6-7, 13
Finance Committee, U.S. Senate, 47
First Amendment, 30
Flying Boxcars, 83

INDEX OF NAMES

Ford, Gerald R., 54, 64
Foreign Affairs, 84
Forest Hills, N.Y., 39, 48-49
Forster, Arnold, 8
Fox, Richard J., 97
Frank, Anne, 92
Frank, Emmett, 25
Freedom Riders, 24
Freedom Seder, 44, 52
Free Speech Movement, 44
French Enlightenment and the Jews, The (Hertzberg), 29
French Revolution, 5
Freud, Sigmund, 5
Friedan, Betty, 63
Friedman, Milton, 60-61

Garcia, Robert, 90
General Assembly, U.N., 20, 50
Genocide Convention, 20
Georgia, 25
Gershfield, Rabbi Edward M., 36, 55
Gittelsohn, Rabbi Roland B., 25
Glazer, Nathan, 50, 93
God, 6, 11, 26, 30, 88
Goldberg, Hillel, 56
Goldbloom, Maurice, 47
Golden Age of American Jewry, 54, 56, 91
Golden Calf, 52
Golub, Rabbi Mark A., 71
Goode, W. Wilson, 3
Goodman, Paul, 7
Gordis, Robert, 74
Graubard, Allen, 4
Gray, William, 90
Great Depression, 8-9, 12, 59, 63
Great Society, 28
Grenada, 79

Haberman, Rabbi Joshua O., 87
Hadassah, 20, 52
Haman, 27
Hanoi, 54
Harlem, 36
Harrington, Michael, 7, 63
Harris, Louis, 67
Harvard Nuclear Study Group, 84
Harvard University, 84
Hatch, Orrin, 75
Hebrew, 4, 14
Hebrew Union College, 11, 89
Hebrew Union College–Jewish Institute of Religion, 53
Helms, Jesse, 75

Hertzberg, Rabbi Arthur, 29, 49, 79
Heschel, Rabbi Abraham Joshua, 18-19, 25-27, 49, 52, 56
High Holy Day Leadership Conference, 82
Himmelfarb, Milton, 47, 83, 92, 97
Hirsch, Rabbi Emil G., 12
Hirsch, Rabbi Richard G., 33-34
Hirsh, Richard, 95
History of the United Synagogue, 1913-1963, The, 16
Hitler, Adolf, 6, 18, 27, 38
Holocaust, 49-50, 73, 93
Honduras, 80
House of Representatives, U.S., 32, 96
Howe, Irving, 7
Human Resources Commission, New York, 58
Hyde, Henry J., 75
"Hymie," 68

ICBMs, 81-82
Indians, 39, 67
Institute for Policy Studies (IPS), 44, 85
Iran, 58, 77
Isaacs, Stephen, 9, 35
Isaiah, 4
Israel, 2, 10, 20, 31, 36-38, 49-50, 52-53, 55-56, 67, 71-72, 81-83, 93-94, 97
Israelites, 44

Jackson, Jesse, 67-68, 70, 97
Jacob, John, 75
JDL, *see* Jewish Defense League
Jefferson, Thomas, 44
Jencks, Christopher, 61
Jewish Community Relations Council, 97
Jewish Defense League (JDL), 48, 56
Jewish Institute for National Security Affairs (JINSA), 87
Jewish Labor Committee, 10, 48
Jewish Liberation Project, 44
Jewish Rights Council, 49
Jewish Theological Seminary, 25, 48, 74, 96
Jewish Values and Social Crisis: A Casebook on Social Action (Vorspan), 40-41, 80
Jewish War Veterans of the U.S.A., 10, 52, 71
Jews for Urban Justice, 44, 52
Jick, Leon, 94
John F. Kennedy Federal Building, 53
Johnson, Lyndon B., 33, 35-36, 51-52
Johnson, Paul, 60-61

INDEX OF NAMES

Joint Advisory Committee on Religion and the State, 29
Joint Commission on Social Action, 20, 25, 33
Joint Committee on Religion and the Public School, 29
Joint Program Plan (NJCRAC), 10, 38, 42, 47, 68, 71
Jones, Leroy, 37
Judaism, 48
Justice, Justice (Cohen), 40

Kahane, Rabbi Meir, 48
Karenga, Ron, 43
Kelman, Rabbi Wolfe, 49
Kemp, Jack, 90
Kennedy, John F., 54
Kennedy, Robert F., 54
Kerner Commission, 36, 42
KGB, 83
King, Jr., Martin Luther, 25-27, 36-37, 52, 54, 67, 70, 76
Kirkpatrick, Jeane J., 79
Korean War, 21
Kotzker Rebbe, 56
Krauskopf, Rabbi Joseph, 12
Krauthammer, Charles, 76-77
Kristol, Irving, 57, 60-61, 93
Ku Klux Klan, 8

Labor Zionists, 52-53
Lamm, Rabbi Norman, 88
Lasch, Christopher, 63
Lear, Norman, 2
Lefever, Ernest W., 88
Left, the, 5, 7, 9, 55, 58, 61, 93, 95
Lehrman, Lewis, 3
Levine, Edward M., 95
Libya, 79
Liebman, Arthur, 43
Liebman, Charles, 94
Lincoln Memorial, 27
Lindsay, John, 47
Lipman, Eugene J., 14, 22
Lipstadt, Deborah, 97
Lithuania, 31
Living With Nuclear Weapons (Harvard Nuclear Study Group), 84
Long Island, N.Y., 82
Los Angeles, 3, 31, 36
Love and Sex (Gordis), 74
Loyola University, 95
Lubavitz Chasidic Movement, 34
Lubell, Samuel, 16

McCarthyism, 21
McCarthy, Joseph P., 21, 23
McCollum v. Board of Education, 30
MacDonald, Dwight, 7
McGovern, George, 3, 47, 97
McWilliams, Carey, 9
Maimonides, Moses, 4, 66
Malcolm X, 37-38
Mandelbaum, Rabbi Bernard, 32
Manhattan, 62
Mantinband, Charles, 25
March on Washington (1983), 69-70
Margolis, Rabbi Morris, 56
Marshall, Louis, 8
Marxism-Leninism, 6, 79-80
Marx, Karl, 5
Mask for Privilege, A: Anti-Semitism in America (McWilliams), 10
Maslow, Will, 8
Math, Rabbi Dennis, 73
Mayer, Egon, 35
Medicaid, 65
Medicare, 64
Megilla (Book of Esther), 27
Messianic Era, 92
Middle Ages, 4
Middle East, 67, 70, 83
Mills, C. Wright, 7
Mississippi, 24
Mondale, Walter, 68
Montgomery, Alabama, 26
Moral Majority, 58, 71-72
Moratorium Day (1969), 52
Moscow, 78
Moses, 26
Mount Vernon, N.Y., 38
Moynihan, Daniel Patrick, 61

NAACP, 61, 64-65
Naked Public Square, The (Neuhaus), 90
Nasser, Gamal Abdel, 38
National Catholic Welfare Conference, 17, 25
National Coalition for Public Education and Religious Liberty, 75
National Community Relations Council, 10
National Conference of Catholic Bishops, 1, 12, 17, 84, 88
National Conference on Religion and Race (1963), 18, 25
National Council of Churches, 1, 12, 17, 25, 33-34, 75, 87
National Council of Jewish Women, 42
National Council of Young Israel, *see* Young Israel

INDEX OF NAMES

National Education Association, 33
National Jewish Coalition, 97
National Jewish Commission on Law and Public Affairs, 34
National Jewish Community Relations Advisory Council (NJCRAC), 2, 10, 18, 28-30, 32, 34, 38, 40-43, 45-50, 64-65, 67-72, 75-76, 78, 83
National Liberation Front, 51
National Opinion Research Center, 54
National Society for Hebrew Day Schools, 34
NATO, 81, 83, 94
Nazi Germany, 23, 26-27
Naziism, 8, 10, 13, 18, 44, 93
NBC News, 97
Negroes, 13, 26, 40, 56
Neshoba County, Mississippi, 24
Neuhaus, Richard John, 58, 90
Newark, N.J., 36
New Deal, 22, 91
Newfield, Rabbi Morris, 13
New Jersey, 30
New Jewish Agenda, 70, 82, 84-85, 87
New Left, 38
New Republic, The, 33, 70, 74, 93
New Right, 58, 71-72
New York, 3, 7, 25, 27, 31-32, 39, 43, 47-48, 52, 60-61, 64, 97
New York State Board of Regents, 30, 33
New York Times, 81, 83, 87, 97
New York University, 38, 42
"Next Steps in the Fight for Equality" (NJCRAC), 46
Nicaragua, 79
Niebuhr, Reinhold, 11
Nixon, Richard M., 46, 52-53
NJCRAC, *see* National Jewish Community Relations Advisory Council
North Korea, 21
North Vietnam, 53-54
Novak, Michael, 60-61
Nussbaum, Daniel, 94-95
Nussbaum, Perry, 25

OAS Charter, 80
Ocean Hill-Brownsville, N.Y., 39
Olympic Games, 78
Oregon, 61
Oregon Law School, 61
Ortega, Humberto, 79
Orthodox Judaism, 4, 14-16, 19, 22, 26-27, 31-32, 34-35, 40, 47-48, 53, 55, 73, 96

Packwood, Robert, 61
Palestine Liberation Organization (PLO), 50, 67, 70, 79
Partisan Review, 7
Pastor, Rodolfo, 80
Pekelis, Alexander, 8-9
Peretz, Martin, 93
Pershing II missiles, 83, 88
Pfeffer, Leo, 9, 29-30, 33
Pharoah, 26
Philadelphia, 3, 12, 36-37, 42, 97
Pines, Burton Yale, 72
Pittsburgh Platform of 1885, 12
Planned Parenthood, 74
PLO, *see* Palestine Liberation Organization
Podhoretz, Norman, 93
Poland, 78
President's Committee on Civil Rights, 25
Preventing the Nuclear Holocaust: A Jewish Response (UAHC), 84
Prinz, Rabbi Joachim, 27
Prohibition, 39
Prophets, The (Heschel), 25
Protestantism, Protestants, 1, 4, 10, 12, 14, 19, 24, 26-27, 29-30, 32, 47, 87
Pruitt, Charles, 97
Public Interest, The, 93
Puerto Ricans, 92

Queens, N.Y., 39

Raab, Earl, 47
Rabbi Isaac Elchanan Theological Seminary, 15
Rabbinical Assembly, 14, 20, 27, 31, 36-37, 42, 49-51, 53, 55, 72-73, 84, 96
Rabbinical Council of America, 15, 22, 24, 29, 40, 53
Racial and Cultural Relations, NCC Department of, 25
Radical Right, 75
Ramparts, 44
Randolph, Jennings, 34
Reagan, Ronald, 3, 58-59, 64, 66, 69-70, 75-76, 78-79, 82-83, 97
Reconstructionist, 94-95
Reconstructionist Movement, 85, 94
Reconstructionist synagogue, 82
Reform Judaism, 11-16, 19-20, 22, 25-27, 33-34, 39-40, 53, 56, 72, 78, 82, 92, 94
Reform Judaism: A Centenary Perspective, 87
Reform Judaism Today (Borowitz), 98
Religious Action Center, 78
Republican party, 3, 21, 92, 97

114 INDEX OF NAMES

Reuther, Walter, 22
Right, the, 3, 55, 58, 61, 77, 91
Rishum, 31
Riverside Church, 52
Roman Catholic Church, 1, 8, 10, 12, 19, 24, 26-27, 29, 32-33, 47, 62, 87
Roman Empire, 92
Rome, 18
Roosevelt, Franklin D., 91
Rosen, Alex, 42
Rosenberg, Harold, 7
Rosenzweig, Franz, 19
Rothschild, Jacob, 25
Rubinstein, Rabbi Richard, 54, 92

Sabbath, 34
Safer Cities Program, 43
Saigon, 54
St. Augustine, Florida, 27
Sakharov, Andrei, 82, 84
Sandinismo, 79
Sandinistas, 79
San Francisco, 17
Saperstein, Rabbi David, 4, 78, 94
Sarna, Jonathan D., 72
SCA, *see* Synagogue Council of America
Scarsdale, N.Y., 49
Schell, Jonathan, 92
Schindler, Rabbi Alexander, 68, 70-71, 73
Schlesinger, Jr., Arthur, 77
Schneerson, Rabbi Menachem, 34
Schrag, Peter, 39
Schulweiss, Rabbi Harold, 41
Security Council, U.N., 21
Segal, Bernard, 25
Selma, Alabama, 26-27, 38
Senate, U.S., 20-21, 27, 47, 61, 73, 75
Sephardim, 11
Shalom Center, 85
Sherer, Rabbi Morris, 34
Sherman, Allen, 24
Sh'ma, 55
Shofar, 52
Siegel, Rabbi Seymour, 5-6, 48-49, 88
Silberman, Charles, 57
Silver, Abba Hillel, 11
Six-Day War, 49, 93
Sklare, Marshall, 16
Slawson, John, 8-9
Smith, Bailey, 71-72
Social Action Commission (Rabbinical Assembly), 14
Social Action Department, NCWC, 25
Social Gospel, 12

Social Security, 64
Soloveitchik, Rabbi Aaron, 27
Solzhenitsyn, Aleksandr, 77, 84-85
Sontag, Susan, 39
South Africa, 78-79
Southern Baptist Convention, 71
Southern Christian Leadership Conference (SCLC), 67, 70
South Korea, 21
South Vietnam, 52, 54
Soviet Jewry, 31
Soviet Union, 6, 21, 31, 50-51, 56, 58, 77-79, 81-85, 89, 93
Sowell, Thomas, 60
Spellman, Francis Cardinal, 32
Spiro, Jack B., 11
SS-20s, 82-83
Star of David, 38
Steinberg, Rabbi Milton, 14
Stern, Marc, 95
Student Non-Violent Coordinating Committee (SNCC), 38
Students for a Democratic Society (SDS), 43-44
Supreme Court, U.S., 23, 25, 30, 32-33, 46, 55, 58, 68-69, 72-74
Synagogue Council of America (SCA), 1-2, 17, 19, 25, 28-30, 38, 40, 45-47, 51, 53, 75-77, 81, 84

Taft-Hartley Act, 22
Talmud, 4, 27, 92
Teheran, 58
Tenafly, N.J., 49
Ten Commandments, 76-77
There Shall Be No Poor (UAHC), 28
Third World, 50, 68, 77
Thoreau, Henry David, 44
Torah, 4, 7, 15, 25, 73
Trident submarine, 85
Truman, Harry S, 22, 25
Two Cheers for Capitalism (Kristol), 93

UAHC, *see* Union of American Hebrew Congregations
Union of American Hebrew Congregations (UAHC), 11, 20-22, 27-28, 33, 38, 42, 48, 51-53, 64, 68-71, 78, 82, 84
Union of Orthodox Jewish Congregations (UOJC), 15, 20, 32, 40, 45, 47-48, 52, 73, 78, 84
United Automobile Workers, 22
United Nations, 17-18, 20-21, 50, 67
United States, 5, 9, 11, 19, 27, 29, 36,

40, 50-52, 54, 56, 67, 78-83, 90, 92-94, 98
United Synagogue of America, 14, 20-21, 25, 27-28, 38, 40, 42, 46, 50, 52, 64, 73, 81
United Synagogue Review, 19
UOJC, *see* Union of Orthodox Jewish Congregations
Urban League, 43, 65, 70, 75

Vatican Council II, 18
Viet Cong, 54, 56
Vietnam, 24, 50-55, 81, 85, 93-94
Vilna, Lithuania, 31
Virginia, 25
Vorspan, Albert, 14, 22, 40-42, 53-54, 66, 68-69, 80, 82

War on Poverty, 28
Warsaw, 44
Washington, D.C., 27, 32, 44, 52, 60, 62
Washington, Harold, 3
Washington Hebrew Congregation, 87
Washington Post, 87, 97
Waskow, Arthur I., 44, 85
Watergate, 97
Watts, 36
Waxman, Rabbi Mordecai, 76
Weimar Germany, 75

We Shall Overcome, 49
White House, 26, 52, 96
White House Conference on Children (1950), 23
Will, George F., 66, 76, 80
Williams, Walter, 60
Wilson, James Q., 62-63, 89
Wilson, William Julius, 60
Wisconsin, 21
Wise, Stephen, 16
Wolfe, Tom, 63
Women's League for Conservative Judaism, 73
Woocher, Jonathan, 97
World Council of Churches, 88
World War I, 57
World War II, 6, 10, 13, 15, 17-18, 23-24, 28, 31, 50-51, 67, 81, 91, 94
World Zionist Organization, 2

Yeshivas, 31-32
Yeshiva University, 15
Yiddish, 7, 15
Yom Kippur War, 49, 83
Young, Andrew, 67
Young Israel, 15, 27, 31

Zion, 4
Zionism, 8, 38, 50
Zorach v. Clausen, 30

CENTER ESSAYS

48. **Who Speaks for American Judaism? Competing Approaches to Public Issues**
   Seymour Siegel, Marshall J. Breger, Joshua O. Haberman, and David Saperstein
   Rabbi Siegel asserts that political liberalism, prevalent in the Jewish community, is true neither to Jewish interests nor to Jewish teachings; he sees signs of a turn toward conservatism. Responses to his theses are offered by a law professor, a leading Reform rabbi, and a religious activist.

49. **Advancing Democratic Principles: A European Examines a Neglected American Asset,** *Stephen Haseler*
   To compete successfully with adversaries of the West in the battle of ideas, Americans should build more effectively on the near universal recognition that the United States is democratic, free, and dynamic, while the Soviet Union is "repressive, bureaucratic, and boring."

50. **Speaking to the World: Four Protestant Perspectives**
   Richard John Neuhaus, Earl G. Hunt, Jr., Paul Ramsey, and Philip R. Cousin
   Lutheran theologian Neuhaus asserts that the current crisis in Christian social ethics is fundamentally a crisis of faith, and that a thorough theological renewal is called for. Responses by a Methodist bishop, a professor of religion, and an African Methodist Episcopal bishop follow.

51. **We and They: Understanding Ourselves and Our Adversary,** *Jeane J. Kirkpatrick*
   An incisive analysis of the worldwide Soviet threat to freedom and a call for the United States to defend itself and Western civilization by military and other necessary measures.

52. **A Tribute to Lech Walesa,** *Ernest W. Lefever, ed.*
   Statements honoring the Polish patriot by President Reagan, Ambassador Jeane Kirkpatrick, Ambassador Max Kampelman, Dr. Zbigniew Brzezinski, Mayor Edward Koch, Governor Thomas Kean, and others, with a message from Walesa.

53. **If East Europeans Could Vote: A Survey,** *Henry O. Hart*
   Opinion research by Radio Free Europe among Eastern Europeans finds a widespread antipathy to Communist regimes (only 4 to 7% of responding Czechs, Hungarians, and Poles support the party) and a strong preference for Democratic Socialist and Christian Democratic systems.

54. **Central America in U.S. Domestic Politics,** *Mark Falcoff*
   The debate over U.S. policies in Central America is more often a reflection of domestic political differences than a realistic appraisal of the region. A Latin American scholar identifies the sources of common errors and points out the real problems we face there.

55. **The Grenada Mission: Crisis Editorializing in the *New York Times*, *Wall Street Journal*, *Washington Post*, and *Washington Times***
   Foreword by Edwin M. Yoder, Jr.; edited by Raymond English
   The fourteen editorials reprinted here, from the two weeks following the landing of U.S. forces on Grenada in October 1983, show a diversity of response, from cheers to unremitting hostility. Veteran journalist Edwin Yoder gives an overview, and an appendix chronicles events on Grenada that led to the U.S. action.

56. **Nuclear Arms and Soviet Aims**
   Ronald Reagan, Pierre Gallois and John Train, Eugene V. Rostow, and Paul H. Nitze
   President Reagan discusses U.S.-Soviet relations; French general Gallois and American writer Train analyze the new trend toward low-yield, high-precision weapons; Yale professor Rostow examines Moscow's nuclear objectives; and chief U.S. medium-range arms negotiator Nitze describes what Moscow means by "peace."

57. **Challenge and Response: Critiques of the Catholic Bishops' Draft Letter on the U.S. Economy**
   Robert Royal, ed.   **$4**
   Responses to the U.S. Catholic bishops' draft pastoral, "Catholic Social Teaching and the U.S. Economy," by the Catholic Lay Commission, Peter L. Berger, Michael Novak, Robert J. Samuelson, Andrew M. Greeley, George F. Will, Charles Krauthammer, and Philip F. Lawler. Historical essay by Archbishop John J. O'Connor.

Essays are $2 each unless marked otherwise. Postpaid if payment accompanies order.
Orders of $25 or more, 10 per cent discount.